LET MY PEOPLE GO

JASON LOZANO

Published by Insight International, Inc.
contact@freshword.com
www.freshword.com
918-493-1718

ISBN: 978-1-960452-03-0
E-Book ISBN: 978-1-960452-04-7

Library of Congress Control Number: 2023918219

Printed in the United States of America.

ENDORSEMENTS

Jason Lozano knows what it means to be set free by God. In his book, *Let My People Go*, he shares his powerful testimony of how he went from a life of hopelessness and bondage to a life of freedom and joy. He also teaches you how to break free from the chains that hold you back and embrace the destiny that God has for you.

Whether you struggle with addiction, depression, fear, or any other issues, this book will show you how to overcome them with God's help. You will learn how to surrender your life to God, how to renew your mind with His word, and how to walk in the power of the Holy Spirit. You will discover the amazing love and grace that God has for you, and how He can turn your mess into a message. This book is not just a book, it's a journey. A journey that will change your life forever. If you are ready to experience the freedom that God has for you, then don't wait any longer. Get this book today and let Jason Lozano show you how to let God's people go!

Rev. Samuel *RODRIGUEZ*
President of the National Hispanic
Christian Leadership Conference (NHCLC)

A young man walked into our Christian rehabilitation center over twenty-five years ago. I never would have imagined what God was going to do with his life. This young man was hungry to change. I would find him crying at the altar month after month. That was the beginning of God changing his life. Throughout the years, he became an evangelist and a preacher at our church. Those who read this book will see the transformative power of God. This young man is now preaching around the world. I am so proud of him.

Pastor Mario *VILLA*
Jason Lozano's Pastor
Shining Light Ministries

CONTENTS

Foreword

Let My People Go is a powerful testimony of the transformative power of God in the life of Jason Lozano. From a life of crime, addiction, and rejection, Jason was set free by the grace of God and has become a powerful leader in the Christian community. This book is a testament to the power of prayer, the power of God's love, and the power of discipleship.

Through his ministry, Jason has helped countless others find their way to God. He has shown them that no matter how broken they may feel, there is always hope for redemption. His message is one of forgiveness, freedom, and love.

Let My People Go is a must-read for anyone who has ever felt lost or alone. It is a powerful reminder that no matter how far we may stray from God, He is always there waiting for us with open arms.

I highly recommend *Let My People Go* to anyone who is looking for hope and inspiration. It is a powerful reminder that no matter how broken we may feel, there is always hope for redemption. Jason's story is a testament to the power of God's love and the transformative power of faith. This book will empower and encourage individuals and churches to walk in the power of Jesus' great commission, "Go and make disciples."

Russell *EVANS*
Senior Pastor, Planetshakers

Introduction

I should've been dead.

My life was in constant chaos.

Drugs controlled me, unforgiveness crippled me, and pain enraged my everyday life.

I was a lost cause, damaged goods.

How could anyone like me ever change? The answer was simple, God.

God took the pieces of my shattered life and restored me.

Have you ever felt alone?

Have you ever been abandoned?

Have you ever felt completely out of control?

Have you ever been bound to addiction?

Have you ever experienced traumatic pain?

If your answer to any of these questions is yes, I wrote this book for you.

Whatever your life may look like, whatever you may have gone through, God can do the unbelievable. God can do the unimaginable.

This book will be a great faith-building lesson for your personal freedom and will help you believe for freedom in the lives of those you love. It will encourage you to believe that God can use even the most broken person and transform that life into a life of value, worth, and purpose.

Allow God to speak to you through my personal story of redemption. I believe that God will meet you right where you are and lift you from whatever pit you find yourself in. I challenge you to open your heart and go on a journey of restoration, healing, and freedom. Trust me, you'll be grateful that you did.

Let My People Go.

1

Far from Freedom

"Hey, son. Would you like to go to a concert with me?"

With that seemingly innocent question, my journey to freedom began. The one asking me the question that day was my mother. Now you must understand, I wasn't normally in the practice of accepting concert invitations from my mom, and I had no idea who would be playing, but I said, "Yeah, sure. I'll go to a concert with you," mainly just to appease her. My thinking at the time was that a concert would at least be a good excuse to do some drugs and party. (Although, in those days, I certainly didn't need a reason to do either!) I asked her, "Will there be a light show?" She responded, "Oh, yes. There'll be a lot of lights, mijo. It'll be great." (In Spanish, the word "mijo" is a term of endearment that means "my son.")

So, by the time the concert rolled around, I was excited about the experience and was looking forward to it. Before heading out the door, I took a bunch of acid hits, also known as LSD, just to enhance the strobe effects of the light show. This was going to be a fun night. But, of course, I had no idea my mom had tricked me. Performing that night was

Carman, one of the most powerful, popular Christian music artists of the day.

"Carman" was actually Carmelo Domenic Licciardello. During the 80s and 90s, Brother Carman's performances were powerful events, with each one charged with a strong anointing of the Holy Spirit. His concerts were bursting with high-energy music and dancing . . . and amazing lights! But more than that, his concerts were filled with a dynamic ministry to all those who were oppressed by the devil. Carman would perform his music in packed arenas and stadiums, proclaiming God's message of freedom over the enemy. His hit song, "The Champion," made it to number one on the charts.

Of course, I was oblivious to all the spiritual stuff going on around me that night. I was high, and all I knew was that the music was awesome, and so were the lights! I was with another girl, and we were both high on acid and enjoying every minute of the concert.

We were partying hard, having the time of our lives, right up until Carman started calling demons out from the stage, urging them to show themselves. That's when the night changed for me. I didn't know what was happening, but I could sense that it was more than just some conjured-up concert theatrics. Something powerful, something real, was happening.

Carman began calling the demons out by name. He called out drug demons, alcohol demons, murder and anger demons, and many others as the Holy Spirit revealed them to him. In the midst of this powerful spiritual warfare, I started to trip out because the demons he was calling out on stage were the same demons inside of me!

As you can imagine, most of my memories of that night are a little hazy. But I do remember this much, in a moment, as fast as you can blink your eyes, I sobered up. That scared me. I'd been high on acid hundreds of times, maybe thousands, and I knew for a fact that you can't just sober up from acid like you can sometimes from alcohol or other drugs. With acid, it takes a full twenty-four hours for the strychnine to work its way out of your body. But, in an instant, I went from being as high as you can get to being as sober as you can get.

That's when I noticed a tear from my eye had started rolling down my cheek. I wasn't used to this. Men, where I came from, just didn't cry. *What the heck is happening to me?* I thought. I felt something I had never felt before, something I'd been looking for all my life. As a young child, my father abandoned me; then, my stepfather abused me. But in that instant, the love of my heavenly Father washed over me like a cleansing shower, setting me free from demonic oppression. It was just that one sweet taste of freedom, and I knew it was exactly what I needed. As others who were there that night told me later, before the altar call was even made, I ran down to the front of the stage and gladly gave my life to God.

LET'S PARTY!

God sent the perfect guy to pray and minister to me that night, a guy I could really relate to. His name was Abraham.

Abraham was a boxer and had a broken nose. He was a rough guy who had been a part of the Italian mob when God got a hold of him and radically saved him. As he told me his story, it was like God used him in a special way to connect with me right there.

Afterward, they took me into the back, to one of the corridors that was blocked off to the public. That's where they surrounded me with prayer warriors and began to drive all sorts of demons out of me. They didn't get them all, but they got a lot of them out that night. I experienced a measure of freedom I hadn't felt since I was a young boy before my dad left.

Then they prayed for me to be born again, and that's when I turned my life over to Jesus. I went home that night feeling like a million dollars. I just felt so good, so different, so free. But just to show you how innocent I was, I called all my friends and said, "Get over here! Bring the keg! Bring the girls and the drugs. Let's party!" They answered, "Why do you want to party?" And I told them, "Because I just got saved! That's why!" I didn't know any better. I just knew I had reason to celebrate, and the only way I knew how to do that was to party!

MOM USES THE FORCE

After about two weeks or so into that new life, my mom came to me and said, "Mijo, you're struggling, huh?" For the first time ever, my mind said one thing, but my spirit, which had recently been reborn, said something else. My mind said, *Don't tell her anything,* but my spirit spoke up for me instead, and I said, "Yeah, I am."

When that happened, I felt like my mom was doing some kind of mind-game voodoo on me, just like when the Jedi Knights used the Force in Star Wars! Then my mom asked me, "And you want to go to a recovery home, don't you?" Again, in my head, I said, *I ain't going to no recovery home. That's just for losers.* But my mouth said, "Yes, I do." Then she said, "If there are no beds, you'd even be willing to sleep on the floor, right?" And I'm thinking, *I'm not sleeping on the floor, you're crazy!* But I said out of my spirit again, "Yes, you're right." So, she said, "Okay, I'm going to get you into a home."

She called a long list of recovery homes before finally finding one that could take me immediately. Like with the Carman concert, the Holy Spirit was conspiring with my mom to make the whole thing happen. I have no doubt I was placed exactly where I needed to be.

Miraculously, I was placed in the same Christian recovery home that two of my old friends had been placed into; one of them I thought had died. I called and talked to them both before I left, letting them know I was headed their way. God was definitely setting me up. It was amazing to be placed in the same facility as a couple of friends of mine. It was truly a miracle.

ENOUGH IS ENOUGH

But before I left for the recovery home, I had an encounter with God that shook me to my core. I was in my room at home smoking speed. I was finishing the last little bit of what I had left in my stash when God spoke to me audibly. Now I don't know if anyone else would have heard Him, but I heard Him as clearly as if He'd been standing in the room with me. You may be thinking, "You were high! The voice you heard was just the drugs talking to you." But here's the deal, I had taken drugs every day for years, and I never once heard God talk to me like He did that day.

He spoke to me in a voice that was loud and clear. There I was, getting high on drugs, and He said, "Mijo, enough is enough." It was God's voice, but I'd heard those words before. Those were the exact words my mother would tell me when she was fed up with my foolish behavior. "Enough is enough." God just repeated that phrase, over and over and over. He must have said it ten thousand times. And every time He said it, it was like ten thousand needles going through my heart.

That was the last day I did drugs. Ever.

THE LOST SON

One of my favorite parables in the New Testament has to be the story of the prodigal son found in Luke 15:11-32. It's such a great picture of the unmerited grace and freedom that comes from a father's love. You know the story. There once was a man who had two sons. One of the sons, the younger one, decided that he wanted to have all of his inheritance at one time. So, he asked his father, who agreed and gave him the money.

With a purse full of gold, the son left home and traveled to a faraway land where he spent his money lavishly, entertaining his friends and buying whatever his heart desired. But there was no way he could sustain that lifestyle, and eventually, he ran out of money. Once out of cash, all of his so-called friends took off, leaving him all alone. The boy was miserable and soon began to starve. He took a job feeding pigs for a local farmer. But soon, the boy was so hungry that the food he was giving to the pigs began to look good to him.

That's when the Bible says that the boy "came to his senses" (Luke 15:17). In other words, the boy finally came to the end of himself; he had hit the very bottom and surrendered. He got to a place where he was so depressed, so oppressed, that he could honestly say to himself the same thing God said to me, "Enough is enough."

Have you ever noticed that the boy never experienced a true change in his life until he came to the end of himself and hit rock bottom? Before reaching that point, he thought he could achieve freedom on his own, by his own power, with his own good ideas. It wasn't until he was able to say "enough is enough" that his journey to freedom was able to begin. He had to come to that place where he'd had enough sin, enough misery, and enough bondage. He was through with it. Enough was enough. Only then did he have his breakthrough and experience freedom in his life.

Meanwhile, do you remember what the father was doing? He desperately wanted his son back. He wanted his son to change, to start making wise decisions instead of foolish ones. He loved him and missed him, and wanted him to come home. He wanted him to be free. The Bible tells us that he eagerly waited and watched for his son every day. But he couldn't make the boy come home. The boy had to make that decision to change for himself. He had to take a step toward freedom. He had to say, "Enough is enough."

What was true with the boy is true for each of us. We need to come to the end of ourselves before change ever happens in our lives. Before we can embark on our own journey to freedom, we need to come to that place where we are so sick of sin that we're willing to do whatever it takes to get free.

How about you? Have you had enough? Are you sick and tired of being sick and tired? Are you willing to do whatever it takes to be free? Then this book is for you. God wants his children to be free. God wants YOU to be free! Free from bondage. Free from sin. Free from oppression from the devil. Are you ready to begin your journey to freedom?

**SCAN QR
FOR MORE
INFORMATION**

2

There's No Place Like Hope

Hope. Just the sound of that word sets off dozens of possible scenarios scrolling through my mind . . .

- *I hope I get the job.*
- *I hope my car starts in the morning.*
- *I hope I get that raise.*
- *I hope my credit card doesn't get declined.*

. . . and some more serious scenarios like . . .

- *I hope my lab work comes back negative.*
- *I hope I don't miscarry this time.*
- *I hope this lump isn't cancer.*
- *I hope God hears my prayers.*

The dictionary defines hope as a feeling of expectation or desire for a certain thing to happen. I suppose that definition is true, but just looking at the words typed out on the page in black and white, the definition seems too sterile, too one-dimensional. I don't know about you, but when I hear the word "hope," I hear a word layered with all sorts of complex feelings and emotions.

Hope, as well as its darker opposite, "hopeless," has been a part of the human experience as far back as history has been recorded. And hope can show up in different forms. To Adam and Eve, hope was an ill-advised bite of fruit. To Abraham, hope was a heaven-sent sacrifice. To Moses, hope was a beautiful land flowing with milk and honey. To David, hope was a sick baby boy needing a touch from God. To John the Baptist, hope was the coming of the Messiah. To Mary and Martha, hope was a resurrection miracle. To Paul, hope was a painful thorn in the side. To the prodigal son, hope was the promise of a loving, forgiving father.

But perhaps the example of hope that touches me most deeply, other than my own story, is the story from the New Testament when Jesus healed the woman in the street (Luke 8:43-48).

A STORY OF HOPE

Picture it with me. It was a narrow, crowded street, and Jesus was being pressed on every side; jostled by a rowdy crowd. He was focused, intent on making it to a house where He needed to see a small girl who was very sick. He was pulled through the crowded streets by the strong chains of compassion placed in His heart by His Creator.

Suddenly, He felt energy, power, strength . . . He felt His essence flow out of Him. He whirled around and asked those with Him, "Who touched me?" But the crowd was perplexed.

EVERYONE was touching Him! They surrounded Him on all sides. He asked again, "No, I mean, who *touched* me?"

Someone did touch Him, and not just His arm or His leg, someone had touched His heart. Someone had touched His destiny, His reason for living. And this someone didn't just touch Him; she actually *drew* from Him. She touched Him with so much need, so much desperation, so much HOPE, that she literally sucked the very power to heal out of Him.

This poor woman, bleeding from some mysterious ailment for many years, lay on the dusty ground before Him. Her head was bowed low, unable to lift her face to look Him in the eyes. She had come to the end of herself. She no longer cared that she would be humiliated. She no longer cared that she'd have to endure the scorn of the crowd for having caused such a delay in the critical visit to see the very sick daughter of a very important man.

For the last twelve years, she'd been unable to be fulfilled as a woman, a wife, a mother. Her life had been about this disease for so long that it had become part of her identity, part of the way she viewed herself, and even part of the way others viewed and referred to her, "Oh, you mean the woman who bleeds?" She had tried everything. Her family had abandoned her, by necessity. She'd drained whatever savings her family had, funds taken by doctors over the years who tried unsuccessfully to heal the unhealable. She had nothing else. She had no other choices. Whatever hope she had was so slight that it hardly existed at all.

Then she heard the crowd; distant at first, but getting closer. She knew something big must be coming her way.

She summoned her courage and began to ask those in front of the procession what was happening. It was then that she heard what was going on. No doubt she'd heard of the Healer before. She knew this could be her chance. She could feel the tiny seed of hope in her heart begin to grow. Throwing caution to the wind, this frail halting woman entered the fray.

She tried to get His attention. She cried out and even tried raising her hands. She tried pitifully to smooth the mess of her hair and wet her eyes so she would look "normal," but in the trying she realized she'd lost "normal" a long time ago. She was most decidedly not normal. She was sick. She was poor. She was lost, almost beyond hope. And it was that desperation that the crowd picked up on, like a stench hanging in the dense air of the crowded street. They curled up their noses and tried pushing her away.

But, as the tiny seed of hope began to grow in her heart, she mustered her strength and jumped, trying to get a better view. She ran ahead in an attempt to anticipate his movements, his route. Her plan was to "lie in wait," intercepting him around the next corner. But it was of no use. The mass of bodies was too thick and moving too fast. She was swept aside by the powerful current of the crowd.

Once passed by, she began to cry. It was over. She'd lost her chance at healing. She would never get better. But somewhere deep inside this poor woman remained a kernel of HOPE. She looked at the crowd moving away from her and found the strength to make one more push. She would try one more time.

Driven by an unquenchable HOPE, she began to pull and tug at the crowd's outer layers. She found the going much easier coming at Him from the back, going with the flow of the people. But her strength waned, and she knew she would not last much longer. She pulled at shoulders and arms and even hair to get to the One she needed to see. She pushed another person to the side and, finally, at once, she recognized the back of the Healer. She focused on His back and reached for Him.

But she got pushed over at the last minute and missed Him. In her desperation she reached out and grabbed the only thing she could reach, the hem of His cloak. She was able to hold on for just a moment but when someone stepped on her arm, she had to let go, finally surrendering to the fact that she would never get better.

But the Healer stopped moving. He turned and she heard Him ask, "Who touched me?" Frightened, she began to push herself away, hoping to blend back into the crowd. But the crowd wouldn't open to let her leave.

She was immediately bathed in warmth, overwhelmed by love. She finally looked up and saw His face. . . no pity there. Just love. Complete and undeniable love. The crowd faded away in her mind and the only two people now in the dusty street were her and this incredible Man.

She felt different, stronger, and stood, weakly at first, but then with a newfound strength. She rose to her full height and looked at the Man in the face. For the first time, she realized fully His piercing gaze. She could not find the words to speak to Him. He simply held out his arms and she rushed into His embrace.

He held her for a long moment. Finally, she pulled away and looked down at her hands, no longer shaking. She felt her toes in the dirt, no longer tingling with loss of circulation. She knew He had accomplished with a touch what many doctors over many years never could. She smiled—for the first time in a very long time—and with that, He smiled back and turned on his heel, once again lost in the current of the crowd.

But the woman was no longer "the woman who bleeds," she had been transformed into *the healed woman*. Everything was new and different. She was made whole; the touch had set her free and made her a new creature.

HOPE BRINGS US TO A DECISION

I love that story. I've always thought that it's such a great example of the power of hope. But the story also illustrates the destructive force of hopelessness. Whenever someone is in bondage to something, there's always an oppressive sense of hopelessness, which is one of the worst feelings imaginable. It saps not only your strength and determination, but it also steals your will to go on. You can find yourself in a very dark place, thinking that there's no light at the end of the tunnel, no brighter days, no better days ahead. I've experienced firsthand this kind of hopelessness, and chances are, you have too.

Hopelessness is what happens when you get beaten down by life. Like the woman in the story, it's a lack of hope that crushes the human spirit. It's my prayer that this book will cause new hope to build in your heart, maybe for the first time in your life. As you read about how God has come through for me, time and time again, I pray that you will be encouraged and that hope would begin to dawn in your heart like a brand-new day.

But with the springing of hope comes responsibility. Hope brings us to an important place of decision. Like the woman in the story, you have to ask yourself, "Am I going to dare to believe again? Am I going to find the courage to step out in faith and allow hope to grow again? Will I ever dream again?" There are choices we each have to make whenever fresh hope begins to emerge in our hearts. Will you say yes again? Is it scary? You bet it is! If you've been disappointed and let down by life, finding the courage to trust in hope again can be a very difficult choice to make.

When I was still a young boy, I was abandoned by my dad. Then, while I was still struggling with that pain and feeling very exposed and vulnerable, I was abused by my stepfather every day. The pain from those wounds crushed me in my spirit. I didn't know who I could turn to for help; I had no idea who I could trust.

A TURNING POINT

I remember the first time I heard Jeremiah 29.11 (NIV), "'For I know the plans I have for you,'" declares the Lord, "'plans to prosper you and not to harm you, plans to give you hope and a future.'" Man, I'm getting emotional just thinking about the power of those words, the power of that promise. Just the thought that God has a plan, that He has a plan for my healing, a plan for my deliverance, my restoration, and my life, completely floors me. Still to this day, reading the words of that verse completely overwhelms me with emotion.

I'm just so very grateful. The first time I heard that verse, I couldn't believe that God would have a plan for me. I thought because of my abandonment and abuse, I was cursed and not eligible for healing. And then I heard my pastor preach a sermon. He read that verse and I heard the words, "God has a plan." And it changed my life forever. Those words are what caused the tiny seed of hope to begin to grow in my heart.

I believe there are a lot of people just like I was, deeply wounded, who have given up on hope, and who don't realize that God has a plan and it's not to harm them and not to hurt them. But His plan is to give them a hope . . . And not just a hope, He also promises a future with plans to prosper and not to harm.

Just think about that for a minute. God has a plan for your life. It sounds so simple, but in reality, it's anything but. It's profound. When I meditate on that truth, that God Almighty, the God of the universe, who created everything, says, "I have a plan for your life," that's pretty heavy stuff.

Hearing that verse for the first time was a real "aha moment" for me. I was a brand-new believer and this was probably one of the very first sermons I'd heard in my life. But in that moment, something inside me clicked and, just like that, I made the decision to go all in. I figured, *If the Bible said it and my pastor said it, it must be true. So I'm going to go ahead and just take a risk and believe it.*

That was a defining moment for me and the beginning of my breakthrough when God floored me with His promise of a good and hope-filled plan for my life. God has a plan. That's such a strong transformational truth. I know it can become cliché for some, but it's not a cliché for me. That single truth in Jeremiah 29:11 changed my life. Since I made the decision to go all in and allow hope to grow again, my life has not just changed, but like the woman in the story, my life has truly been transformed. This book contains not just the stories of my transformation journey, but also the lessons I learned along the way.

My story, just like everyone else's, is full of heartache and pain. But praise God, Jesus Christ is the Redeemer, the Restorer, the Deliverer, and He never leaves us like He found us. He is faithful and my life is a testimony to that fact.

3

A Life Shattered

Being abandoned by my father is one of the earliest memories I have. I was only six or seven years old, around that age, when my mother and father decided to divorce.

In 1978, four-year-old Jason with his mom and sister.

Left:
Five-year-old Jason at his dad's farm.

Right:
Jason Lozano in first grade.

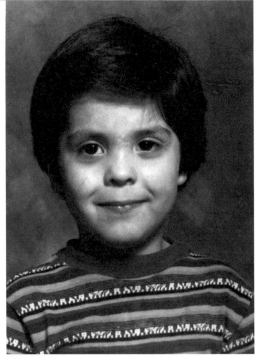

From my understanding, before the divorce, my father was being trained to be a pastor. But his training was interrupted when he was drafted to fight in Vietnam, where he became what they called a "tunnel rat." Tunnel rats were soldiers who performed underground "search and destroy" missions in enemy territory.

While he was over there fighting, he saw things and did things that he never talked about, horrific things that impacted him negatively. Not surprisingly, he became addicted to all kinds of stuff, and when he finally came back from the war, he just wasn't the same. My parents' marriage couldn't survive the addictions and eventually dissolved. As a result, my dad fell fully into his alcoholism.

My mother got custody of my sister and me while my brother went to live with my grandma. And so, on the weekends, I would go to my father's house where he lived out in the country on a ranch. I have some good memories of going to my dad's house at that time. We'd have so much fun. There were always kids at the ranch and there weren't a lot of rules or supervision—just kind of like wild ranch living.

And then, right around Christmas time one year when I was just about six or seven years old and after a weekend full of fun at the ranch, my father dropped me off at my mom's house loaded down with a bunch of presents for everybody. I remember all of it so clearly. I got out of his car in front of the house, and he said to me, "Okay, son, I'll see you next weekend." I remember the days that followed crept by slowly. I thought the weekend would never arrive. So, when the next weekend finally came around, I was outside waiting for him with my little backpack all packed up and ready to go. I waited for what seemed like an eternity. He never showed up.

He didn't show up the next day either, or the day after that, or the day after that. After about a week, I'm not sure how long it was, but at some point, when he still hadn't stopped by or called, my mom finally had to tell me, "I don't think your dad is coming to get you." Those words, and the realization my dad wasn't coming to get me, broke my heart. Something on the inside of me shattered that day. I remember that distinctly. I just kept asking myself, *What did I do wrong?* My feelings were all over the map, and a whole gamut of thoughts swirled through my mind.

A LIVING NIGHTMARE

By that time, my mom had gotten a new boyfriend, and in the midst of my pain and desperation, I turned to this man to be a father figure in my life. But, just like my own dad, this new guy was an alcoholic too and he would drink every day. And whenever he'd drink, he'd get very abusive. He began to abuse me every single day. He would beat my mom in front of me. It was just a terrible environment to grow up in; a living nightmare. And I lived in that nightmare throughout my childhood.

Things always got worse during the holidays. He would literally grab the tree from inside the house and throw it outside onto the yard. He'd do this every year. Whenever there was a Christmas or Thanksgiving dinner with expensive china on the table, he'd shatter all the dishes and make a mess of the table. It was just how he was. He was also a gun collector; he liked his guns so much that he would sit in his chair in the middle of the night and shoot the guns off in the house!

It was literally like living with a crazy man. Looking back, it's easy to see that he was a very, very evil man. My mom told me later that when he found out she wanted to go to church, he put the barrel of his biggest pistol in her mouth and said, "If you go to church, I'll blow your head off." And I'm convinced that he would've done it. He was a womanizer and an abuser; he was just a terrible man. And he became my father figure, so you can just imagine the kind of toxicity present in the environment I was raised in.

A PIVOTAL CROSSROADS

The thing is, I was always a good-hearted kid. I knew the Lord as a little boy because my mom sent us to children's church. I had given my heart to the Lord at church at a young age. I always knew the Lord, and I always feared Him, so there was always that spiritual side of me, but then I became a teenager.

When I was about twelve years old, my mom took me to a revival meeting taking place at a church just down the street. There was a powerful lady at the revival praying for people who went down front to the altar. As she would pray for them, they would fall over. I started making fun of them, saying, "That's so fake. What are those people doing?" My mom quickly responded to my skepticism, "You think it's fake?" I said, "Yeah." She said, "Okay, why don't you go up there and see for yourself."

So, I made my way to the altar, where the lady prayed for me. The next thing I knew I was on the floor just like the others! I quickly realized, *Whoa, what the heck?! This really is real!* I felt like the room was spinning. I got up and began to walk out of the church. On the way out, I passed by the youth room which was full of young people. They all turned and stared at me, but they didn't invite me in to join them. It was like I didn't belong there.

So instead of going into that youth room—which, looking back, was a pivotal crossroad at a critical time in my life—I kept walking. It's interesting to think about what might have happened at that moment because I believe if I had gone into that youth room, my life would have been a whole lot different. But they didn't invite me in, so I kept walking down the hall and out of the building. Once outside, a girl back behind the church named Tina caught my eye. She was a wild girl, and we shared a joint, my very first one. From that moment on, it was like I had turned my back on God. The next seven years were like seven years of tribulation. Everything just went from bad to worse.

CRAZY YEARS OF TRIBULATION

It was around my freshman year of high school when I really started getting mischievous, hanging with the wrong crowd, getting into trouble, and just looking for ways to misbehave. I eventually got expelled from every school in the district for always getting suspended. Things turned even more serious when I was fourteen years old. I committed a small robbery and was shipped off to youth prison.

Above:

Jason Lozano's mom at her college graduation at Rio Hondo College.

Left:

Jason Lozano, Pioneer High School graduation.

Jason Lozano, eighteen years old.

Jason Lozano in youth prison.

A Life Shattered

All my other friends were going to high school, playing football, having fun, and hanging out, and I was being shipped off to prison. And I found that I had stepped into a whole different kind of world.

Prison is a different kind of a nightmare because, at that time, I wasn't a hardened criminal. I was thrown in with a bunch of young, hardened kids who'd been institutionalized. So, I had to learn a whole new way of thinking. Youth prison felt like a gladiator school where Satan himself trained young people. That's where I first learned how to move like a gangster with a gangster mentality. I had to adapt to survive inside.

That year in youth prison changed the course of my life. By the time I got out, I was a different person. My whole mindset had shifted. I had accepted the fact that I was a troublemaker. Even when I tried to walk a straight narrow line, I failed. I was too messed up and couldn't keep from getting into trouble. One thing led to another, and I ended up doing more than just taking drugs; I began selling them. Soon I became the second-largest drug dealer in our area. I sure did some crazy things in that world, but that's the state of mind I was in.

An example of how crazy it became was one time this girl asked me to sell her some drugs. And I couldn't help but notice she had this big diamond ring on her finger, so I decided to steal it from her. But I didn't have a weapon. So, when I took her to the place to get the drugs, I went in and asked the guys there, "Do you have any weapons? I want to rob this girl." They said no, but they did have a butcher knife I could use. So, I said, "That'll work. Do you have a mask?" They said, "Yes, we have a mask." They had one of those scary clown masks. So, I put on the mask, got the knife ready, and prepared to go back outside to rob the girl.

Now you have to understand that I never wore a shirt at this point in my life. I guess I thought I was buff or something. So, I went back outside, wearing that silly clown mask, and pointed a big butcher knife at the girl and tried to take her ring. She screamed, "Jason, is that you?" And I'm like, "How do you know it's me?" I had completely forgotten that I had a tattoo of my name right there on my chest! It was obvious to the girl who was trying to rob her!

GOD'S HAND OF PROTECTION

Then there was the time that I spent my eighteenth birthday in a Mexican prison. This was a scary experience, to say the least. I'm Mexican, but I don't speak Spanish, and that's looked down upon in Mexico. They would call me "pocho" which stands for a Mexican American who doesn't speak Spanish. So, needless to say, those guys didn't like people like me. In fact, they would rape and kill people like me! But somehow, God protected me. During that time, God's strong hand of protection was undoubtedly on my life.

My friend and I were in that Mexican prison together and I remember having to sleep back-to-back to protect ourselves. So many guys had knives in there, and they could just kill you if they wanted to. It was so scary. I didn't show it, but I was scared for my life almost the whole time. It was just a terrible place, like a scene from a Hollywood movie where they throw you into a room and say, "Take a shower!" But they just leave you with a bucket of dirty water to wash yourself and a set of dirty clothes to put on.

It was just a crazy experience in that prison. I remember when this one guy came into the prison. He was a drug lord of some kind, and he practically had a condominium, living in that prison like a king. He was from Long Beach, California, the same area I was from. He told me, "Don't worry, no one will hurt you here. I'm going to take care of you." And sure enough, that's what happened. God used that drug lord to watch over and protect us. So the whole week we were in the Mexican prison, no one hurt us, no one even touched us. I'm sure there were guys in there who wanted to kill us, but they didn't try anything because we were being protected by the drug lord (not to mention the Lord of Lords!).

The whole time I was in that place, I was so scared. I was continually haunted by the thought, *I'm never getting out of here.* Then, out of nowhere, God did another miracle. The guy I got arrested with, my friend, his grandfather was an ex-Federale in Mexico. Evidently, my friend's parents talked to his grandpa, and he was able to pull some strings and get us released. So one day, after we'd been there about a week, they just opened the gate and let us go!

Of course, I assumed that if they let us go, they would probably shoot us, making it look like we were trying to escape. The guards were armed with AK-47s and could have easily shot us once we were outside the gate. So I told my friend, "You run to the left; I'll run to the right." But when we got outside the gate, no one tried a thing. What a miracle that was! My mom and dad were even there to pick us up! I left Mexico saying, "I'm never going back!"

One of the reasons I was afraid I would never get out of that prison was because they would perform drug tests to see if you had drugs in your system (that was just one thing that they would do to incriminate you). So, one of the things I did was actually drink the water out of the toilet so I could pass the drug test. Not surprisingly, I ended up getting very sick with dysentery.

As I said, when I got home, I vowed never to go back to Mexico. But just a week later, my friends showed up saying, "Let's go back to Mexico to party," but I told them, "I ain't never going back to that place." When they started taunting me, saying, "Come on, come on, you sissy!" I finally said, "All right, let's just go." So, I went back to Mexico just one week later. Can you believe I got in a bar fight and ended up back in that same prison? That's just the kind of crazy mentality I had at that time in my life. It wasn't rational.

A PEACEFUL ENDING

During those days, I was a fighter. I loved boxing, and I was really good at it. I was at this hamburger place, and this rival gang, well known in that area for burning people alive, was there. These guys were real life gangsters, part of organized crime, a bunch of hardened criminals. They were notorious in the region for their brutality. One of the guys came out of the hamburger joint and started walking in my direction. I saw him and called him out. I wanted to fight him, so I jumped him and beat him up. I even did the Muhammad

Ali Shuffle over him just to rub it in. (I was drunk and just being silly). What I didn't know was about eighteen other gang members had seen the whole thing and were all about to walk out of that hamburger joint!

When they came outside, I realized I would probably die anyway, so I ran straight toward the biggest one. I hit and beat him. The fight attracted the attention of the security guards, who ran out of the restaurant and started spraying mace at me. Then the gang members pulled their guns out, and the guards pulled their weapons out. There was a stand-off right there in the parking lot.

Meanwhile, even though I could barely see because of the mace, I ran inside the restaurant to the bathroom to hide. I immediately started to pray as I had never prayed before, "God save my life! I have no weapon. These guys are going to come in here and kill me at any moment!"

But they never came for me. The standoff outside ended peacefully, with everyone putting their weapons away without firing a shot. Everyone just went their separate ways. I guess in all the excitement, they had forgotten about me. That night God definitely spared my life. But that's the kind of condition my life was in and those were the kind of things that happened in my life all the time.

MORE POWERFUL THAN ORGANIZED CRIME

Eventually, I became the largest drug dealer in the city. And I connected with a couple of methamphetamine cooks so my drug business could grow even more. One of the guys was a motorcycle gang member and the other was a professional bounty hunter. I was still a young kid, only eighteen or nineteen when I started manufacturing methamphetamine in the city. I took over drug houses and the whole nine yards, becoming a major player in the area even though I was still young.

Things in my life were already dangerous, but they ramped up when organized crime decided that we had to pay an extra fee to the boss over our region if we sold drugs. When that happened, I decided I didn't want to pay extra to anybody, so that's when we ended up going to war with organized crime. A lot of my friends died during that time. It was madness. Eventually, I got placed on a hit list. And so, by the time I got saved that night at the Carman concert, I was a wanted man with my name on a hit list.

But God's destiny for my life was more powerful than any of that stuff. During those years, God's hand of protection covered me, protected me, and kept me from death countless times. Remember the verse Jeremiah 29:11, "'For I know the plans I have for you,'" says the Lord. "'They are plans for good and not for disaster, to give you a future and a hope.'" Never forget that God's plan for you is far greater than any plan the devil may have for you. Let my story encourage you. Like He did for me, God has a plan for your life. A plan to give you a future and a hope!

4

The Power of Fervent Prayer

I've always loved the second half of the verse James 5:16. It says, "The prayer of a righteous person is powerful and effective" (NIV). This is another great promise from God. I've never had to wonder whether that verse is true or not. I know for a fact that I'm alive today because of the powerful prayers of a committed group of prayer warriors who covered me with fervent prayer in the days and weeks just before I got saved.

At the time, my mom had met a man named

Mom and Stepdad at their Bible College graduation in 1997.

Dwayne and they ended up getting engaged and married. To this day, I refer to him as my dad.

My mom and dad were attending Bible college where they were serving God together. I was living with them at the time. And this team of prayer warriors would call my mom, telling her they were praying for me. They did this all on their own without my mom even having to ask. There were six or seven of them on the prayer team, and within twenty-four hours, each of them had called my mom telling her, "We need to pray for Jason because the spirit of murder and death is over him." They had no idea what I was doing or what I was involved with. It was God having people pray for me. Another miracle!

Days passed until one day I was awakened out of a dead sleep by a detective who had barged into my bedroom at about 5:00 or 6:00 in the morning. He pulled me up out of bed, slapped cuffs on my wrists, and arrested me on embezzlement charges. I knew I was guilty and was probably looking at ten years or so in prison for the crime.

So, I was in the county jail being arraigned, and I was looking at my court dates for the charges. I read through all the evidence they had stacked up against me. That's when I knew I was going to prison for a long time. Maybe a week later, while I was still in jail, the police raided my mother's home with eighteen cop cars and a helicopter hovering overhead. They were looking for me on some drug charges I didn't even know about. They didn't realize I was already in custody in the county jail.

The cops broke down the door and rushed into the house. They found my mom and dad and immediately put guns on them. Now, keep in mind, these two were in Bible college, studying hard and believing for my salvation. That's the only thing they were "guilty" of. The cops also found my sister and my baby niece. My sister was a drug addict, so they placed her down on her knees. The cops got them all on the floor while they searched the house for drugs or cash.

The reason they raided the house was because I had allegedly sold drugs to an undercover cop. I didn't know about this allegation at the time. They searched all over but didn't find anything to support the allegation, and they were not happy. The reason they didn't find any drugs was because God did a miracle on my behalf.

Just before the raid, I was sitting in my jail cell with a Bible in my hands, just praying to God to help me, and He did. He told me, "The police are coming to your house. Get the drugs out now." So, I called a friend and told him to hurry over to my mom's house and get the drugs out. I told him, "You can keep the money and the drugs. Just make sure I get the money when and if I ever get out of here."

Well, barely twenty minutes after he left my mom's house with the drugs, the cops came busting in. If they had found those drugs in the house, I know I would have never gotten out of prison. It was the mercy of God that saved me that day.

I was thankful that they didn't find the drugs, but the fact was, I was still in jail on embezzlement charges, and I was beyond guilty. They had all the evidence they needed to lock me up and throw away the key, but this is the part I still don't understand to this day. What had happened with those embezzlement charges can only be described as a miracle. I have no idea why or how this happened, but one morning around 2:00 a.m., the police just opened the door and let me walk out of jail! Usually, the only way you get out like that is if you snitch or give up names, but neither of those things happened. They just let me out with no court date, nothing. They opened the door, and they let me out. I called a taxi and went home. I couldn't believe it; it was almost like Paul and Silas in the Bible (Acts 16:16-40). To this day, I still don't know why I was released like that. All I can figure is that God was answering those women's prayers and moving in my life. It was unbelievable. The whole thing was just a miracle.

When I got out, I went straight to my mom's house. I felt really bad about the cops raiding my mom's home and tearing up the place; I just felt really bad about the whole thing. She was obviously upset; the doors were broken and damaged, and the whole place was a wreck following the raid. But she was trying to walk in the love of God toward me because she was a woman of faith. Along with my dad, they were faithful to get up every morning at 5:00 a.m., and pray over me, speaking the Word of God over me.

I knew that their prayers were powerful because whenever they prayed, I could see something like smoke coming under my bedroom door. I'd be getting high in my room, and the smoke would filter in under the door and fill up the entire room. I knew by intuition that if that smoke touched me, it would weaken me. So whenever that would happen, I'd just jump out of the bedroom window to get away from it. Every morning for an hour and a half, sometimes two hours, my parents would speak the Word of God over my bedroom door. Looking back, I know that while I slept, the glory of God would rest on me because of those fervent prayers.

"I'M COMING AFTER YOU NOW!"

In those crazy days, before going into the recovery home, God was letting me know that He was not giving up on me, no matter what. I remember buying a 1967 Ford Mustang, it was my pride and joy. One time I left the Mustang at the house of one of the drug dealers who cooked for me.

The next morning, I was on my way back to the house to pick up the car when I got a phone call from the police station that somebody had hit my Mustang! So I hurried over to the house, shouting at God the whole way, "Leave me alone! I know You did this! Why don't You just leave me alone?" I pulled up to the house, and low and behold, the police were right. My Mustang was rammed up against a tree in the front yard!

A little Ford Pinto had hit the Mustang, lifting it up, bending the frame, and smashing the front of the car into a tree. I could see right away that it was totaled. The cops on the scene told me that the lady driving the Pinto had escaped from a mental hospital in Oregon. She escaped in the Pinto, drove for over fifteen hours, then hit my car that was sitting in front of the cook's house. Talk about random!

There is no doubt in my mind that it was God trying to get a hold of me. What is the likelihood of a crazy lady escaping from a mental hospital in Oregon in a Pinto, of all the cheap cars, ending up in L.A., and destroying my 1967 Mustang? It was just like God was saying, "Enough is enough! Your life as you know it is over. I'm coming after you now!"

THE OLD LIFE ENDS, A NEW ONE BEGINS

After some calling around, my mom finally found a home that had some space for me. So I packed my clothes and got ready to go to my friend's house; he was going to give me a ride. He had just graduated from the home and was on his way to church, which is where the home was.

I showed up at his house with my clothes literally stuffed in a trash bag. None of my clothes fit, by the way, because all I wore at that time were baggy gang member clothes. Here I was, a size 28, wearing size 44 pants. It sounds ridiculous now, but that was the style back at that time.

So we're hanging out at my friend's house, and he's telling me the rules of the home. He's telling me you can't listen to worldly music, you can't do this, you can't do that, and all these things that I was obviously doing. I just said, "Okay, whatever." Then he told me, "Make sure you tell the pastor that you're going to be there for six months. I know you're just planning on being there for thirty days but tell him six months because that's the program's rule. If you tell him thirty days, they're not going to let you in."

In my mind, I was just going to this program to clean up a little bit, get my head straight, work out . . . almost like a prison kind of mentality, and then after thirty days I'd leave.

I had no intention of cleaning up completely or serving God at all.

As we started driving to the home, there was a hill called Colima we had to drive over to get to the church. You can really see all of Los Angeles from the top of that hill. We were driving up the winding road in the car with my friend's girlfriend, and I remember thinking what a miracle that was. I realized God was doing something powerful in this guy's life. We were going to church with his girlfriend! That made absolutely no sense to me based on the world I had been living in.

As we were going up the hill, I looked back down at the city lights of L.A., and in that moment, I realized that my life was not just changing, my old life was over. As we went over the hill and descended into the city of La Puente, I knew I was entering into a whole new life.

EVERYTHING'S GOING TO BE OKAY

We pulled up in front of a building that looked like an old warehouse. I was shocked when I found out that old building was the church! I didn't know a lot about what churches were supposed to look like, but I didn't think they were supposed to look like a warehouse. Everything seemed so strange to me. As I stepped in, I thought, *What the heck is this place? And what about this music and all this dancing? This is really weird.* That's when my friend Billy came up to me, and he was dancing.

The last time I'd seen Billy, he was pale and emaciated, looking like the walking dead. Now here he was, looking like an angel. He was handsome, bright, in shape, with God's glory all over him. Plus, he was dancing! I was startled when I saw him because he was just beaming with the light of God. Just seeing Billy like that broke off my pride and my bad attitude about what was happening all around me. Immediately, I felt the presence of God, and then I knew that everything was going to be okay.

After the service was over, I went up and talked to the pastor who ran the home and told him I would be staying for six months. It was good because I really felt like I had a connection with him. He was the founder of the Mongols. The Mongols and Hells Angels are probably the two biggest biker gangs in the region, maybe in America. The pastor was a very large, scary-looking man. He was like 6'6"; he was a big, massive man. I could just feel that he had a lot of love, but at the same time, I knew not to mess with this guy. But I felt like he loved and understood me. Little did I know that I wouldn't stay in the home for thirty days, or even for six months. I was in that home for five years. Five years of learning how to walk with God and how to seek His face every single day.

I've been so blessed throughout my life and to be where I am today is really unbelievable. When I think back over my journey and all the times that God rescued me out of a terrible situation, or helped me learn a valuable life lesson, or protected me from the enemy's attacks, it's incredible and I'm so grateful.

As we close out this chapter, I just want to remind you that God is always with you too, just as He's been with me throughout my whole life. He has promised that He will never leave us, nor forsake us (Deuteronomy 31:6). Whatever trial you may be going through, I can promise you that He is right there with you. He has a beautiful plan to save you, redeem your life, and set you free.

SCAN HERE TO LISTEN TO PASTOR VIRGINIA'S TESTIMONY ON THE POWER OF FERVENT PRAYER.

5

Conversations with God

I'm taking the time to share so many of my stories with you because I want you to see how God was with me every step of the way, no matter how crazy things got. Through it all, He never left me. He never turned his back or gave up on me. He was always there to lovingly draw me back to his side, patiently teaching me about His nature and the nature of His Kingdom. One of the first things He taught me was how to pray.

LEARNING HOW TO PRAY

I walked into the home that day still high on methamphetamine. I knew I was going to get clean, but I wanted to use the last of my stash before heading to the recovery home. I pretty much slept through my first few days there. I remember the daily schedule at the home was very regimented, just like being in the military. They were building a new discipline into my life, something I had never had before.

It was rise and shine every morning at 6:00 a.m.! I'd have to wake up, brush my teeth, wash my face, and then head straight to prayer. The leaders would announce to the group, "Okay, now it's time to pray . . . for one hour." I had really only prayed early in life, and even then, it was just a few sentences at a time. I had no idea how to pray for a few minutes, much less a whole hour. They would turn the lights down in the room, and everyone would start praying in the Spirit, and it would get pretty crazy, real Pentecostal. The guys would all just start shouting out to God, all at the same time. There were forty-seven ex-drug addicts in that room praying together. It was powerful stuff.

I didn't know what the heck was going on. So, I just got on my knees and prayed my first, simple, tentative prayers like, "Oh God, help me stay sober." "Oh God, forgive me of my sin." That was it. That was all I had. So I used the rest of the time to go back to sleep. When the prayer time was over, and they turned the lights back on, they saw me lying on the floor asleep, and asked me, "How are you? You okay?" I was like, "Oh yeah, I'm fine. Let's pray some more; I'm still tired!"

But later, little by little, day by day, I learned how to pray for five minutes, then for ten minutes, then for fifteen minutes, and then for twenty-five minutes. Eventually, I learned to pray for a full hour. I've exercised that prayer muscle now to the point where I can pray for eight or nine hours at a time. So when the Lord calls me to do that today, it's not a problem. But it all started with a little, tiny prayer.

I teach a lot about prayer at our church. I always say, "An hour of prayer a day keeps the devil away." So, if you want to pray for an hour but don't think you can, don't be discouraged if it's for five minutes or ten minutes or whatever; little by little, you'll get better at it.

In my mind, I was still on a thirty-day journey, thinking I'd leave when the month was up. But then somewhere in those thirty days, I started having powerful encounters with God. I decided maybe I'd stay ninety days. Then eventually, I ended up staying for five years.

A DECEPTIVE WORD

I made friends with a guy from the neighborhood. He was a bright guy, but wild, like a prodigal child. He was in the home so he could recover from his addiction to drugs and cocaine. I liked him and we got pretty close. He was a sharp guy, a cool guy.

I could tell he had a gift from God. But he would dabble in the occult and often used his gift in a perverted way and for the wrong things. He was in the Kingdom of God, trying to do what was right, but he had what I know now as a familiar spirit, which is when a demonic force controls you. It's strange when you're not right with God, like people who do palm reading and all that. A lot of them have a gift from God, but they've allowed it to become corrupted by the enemy.

Anyway, he's telling people things and reading palms, which you weren't allowed to do, but he was sneaking around, doing it on the side. I got curious and asked him, "What are you doing?" He told me, "Oh, I'm just telling people about their future and stuff." I was fascinated and wanted to hear more. He said, "Let me see your ID. Let me see your hand."

I handed over my ID and let him see my hands, and he said, "Tonight in the revival service, the speaker is going to call you up onto the stage. He's going to tell you that God has called you into the ministry."

Sure enough, that night came, and we all went to the service together. The place was packed with around four to five hundred people. Even before the service began, I could tell that the anointing was strong that night; the power of God was there. The speaker was a powerful man of God; I'd seen this guy raise people right out of wheelchairs. His name was Philip LaCrue, an evangelist who was very strong in the anointing. He has gone to be with the Lord now, but he was very powerful back in the day.

Right in the middle of his sermon, he called me out of the crowd, saying, "Young man come up here!" He pulled me onto the stage, looked me in the eyes, and said, "The Spirit of God says to you, 'God has called you into the ministry. You're going to preach the gospel all over the world.'"

I don't remember this, but I was told later that when he prayed for me, I went flying: I was knocked down by the power of the Holy Spirit. There was no one standing behind me to catch me, so I just flew backward when he touched me. The power of God hit me and wrecked me. To think that God not only thought about me but also had a plan for my life, completely overwhelmed me. I was shocked. I answered the call of God right there. I told God, "Yes. I'll do it. I'm ready."

I returned to the home after the service floating on air. I was super excited. I woke up the following day and the first thing I wanted to do was talk to my friend again. Now, keep in mind that he's still recovering from drugs. So I asked him, "Hey, do you have any other words from God for me?" He answered, "Yes, yes, I'll give you another one." It was weird; this guy could flow in and out of the Spirit just like that. First, he'd be in the Spirit, and then he would be in the flesh. But at the time, I was too young and immature in the Lord to discern what he was doing, which was a problem. The first word he gave, the one about me being called into the ministry, was a word of wisdom, and it was spot on. But the next word he gave was a deceiving word. He told me, "You are going to fall over a woman, but you're going to come back stronger than ever." And I said, "Wow, okay."

Not knowing any better, I started packing my bags. I wanted to hurry up and fall and come back because I wanted to serve God. One of the staff looked at me and asked, "What the heck are you doing?" I replied, "Oh, I'm going to fall and come back because I want to serve God." He looked at me like I was crazy. He said, "What are you talking about?" Then he took the Bible and opened it up to the scripture where it says that God can keep you from falling. When I saw that, it was a revelation. It blew up in my spirit. I thought, Wait a minute, that guy lied to me! I realized just how close I had come to losing my life. If I would've fallen, I would have never come back. I confronted this guy, "Hey, why would you do that to me?" Then he manifested and started cussing me out. That's when I blanked out.

It's tough to explain exactly what happened to me. Maybe the best way is to use the example of the man in the Bible who was demon-possessed. He was the man who Jesus cast the legion of demons out of and who had super-human strength (Mark 5:1-20). I believe that's a true story because the same thing would happen to me from time to time; I would have superhuman strength. I don't know how to explain it theologically. I'm just telling you what happened to me.

ANOTHER MIRACLE FROM GOD

The guy was really going crazy, cussing me out, and something in me just snapped. I grabbed a heavy metal bunk bed, like an army bunk bed, and threw it across the room. Then I slugged the guy in the head. He went flying through a window and broke the glass with his head. I thought, *Oh, man, this is it. I've seen this same thing happen a hundred times. He's going to pull his head out of the window and he's going to be all cut up. He's going to be hospitalized and I'm going to prison.* I was on probation then, so I was ready to grab my bags and run to Mexico. But the guy pulled his head out of the window and didn't have a scratch on him.

Then something happened to me—and this is how I knew I was genuinely saved—I felt awful for what I had done. That feeling was new for me. I had never felt bad for hurting anybody before; I would actually rejoice in it. But that's how I knew the Holy Spirit was working on me. I ran straight into the bathroom and started crying out to God, "God, why am I like this? Why did I blank out again? I'm a Christian now; I'm no longer supposed to do that. Why did

I blank out like I used to?" This is where God was teaching me about deliverance.

Obviously, they were supposed to kick me out of the home; those were the rules. You can't be fighting in the home like that. It's an automatic dismissal. As I was called into the office, I was praying for mercy the whole time. I didn't want to leave, especially under those circumstances. I was heart-broken about it. I told Pastor Andy, "I don't know what's wrong with me. I don't know. I just blanked out. Something's wrong with me."

That's when God performed another miracle. The Holy Spirit spoke to Pastor Andy, saying, "If you kick Jason out, he's going to die. You need to give him a second chance." So, he said, "I've never done this. I've run this home for years and have never done this. But God's telling me right now I need to give you another chance. So, I'm going to give you another chance. But you're going to have thirty days of discipline."

For thirty days, I had to clean all the dishes for forty-seven men. These are big pans and heavy dishes, like army dishes, hundreds of them. It took hours. I'd start after dinner and be working in the dreaded dish pit until midnight. By the time I was done, I was wet, cold, and miserable. But it was better than being kicked out of the home.

A LESSON IN FORGIVENESS

Though I didn't realize it at the time, I was practically paralyzed by anger and unforgiveness in my life. One time a director on the staff called me on it. He came up to me while I was washing dishes. This guy was used by God in my life a lot in those early years, but he could also be very antagonistic and carnal at times.

He was a big Samoan guy. He'd been in about ten different homes. He figured out how to go into homes and stay there for years, do good, backslide, then go back into another home. It was his routine. He came up to me and said, "How are you doing, brother?" with a cocky voice, just trying to get under my skin . . . and it was working. I could feel that old familiar anger coming on me again. I said, "Count it all joy, brother." I wasn't trying to be nice by quoting scripture; I was basically telling him, "I'm going to hit you."

I started to grab a pan to whack him in the head with it, but he saw what I was doing, and the next thing I knew God was using him in a mighty way. "You know what, Jason, I'm going to tell you something," he said, de-escalating the situation. "You need to go in that room right now." It was the prayer room next to where we were. He said, "You need to go in that room, and you need to go forgive your dad."

Well, he knew absolutely nothing about my dad. But when he told me that, the whole room started spinning. I felt like Mike Tyson had just punched me in the gut because I was about to get delivered. His words hit me at the core of my pain. He then told me, "Don't worry about the dishes. We will get somebody else to do them for you. You just need to get in that room." So I went into the prayer room and got on my knees. I must have been there for three or four hours, forgiving people from my past whom I had never forgiven, starting with my father.

Forgiving him was an excruciating thing to do because I loved my dad, and I still do. I just had to let his abandonment go. I was close to my dad when I was a little guy. He would always take me fishing. I knew my dad. I had great memories of us together. But then, after that, he left me, breaking my heart. I was shattered. I had to let all of that go, and it was hard, but I did it.

Then I had to forgive the next person, who was my stepfather. This one was extra difficult because he abused me when I was a boy. Unless you've been through it, there's no way you can understand what it's like to be abused every day. It's insane. It's like being in a mental hospital with crazy people. You're living in an insane environment. It destroyed my soul. But God said, "You need to forgive him." So I called him by name and said what he did, and then let it go.

Next, I forgave my stepsister for abusing me too. Then I had to forgive my stepbrother because he used to bully me. As I was saying prayers of forgiveness, the Lord told me the next person I needed to forgive, which shocked me. The Lord told me to forgive my mother. It surprised me because, in the Hispanic culture, your mother is right there next to sainthood; You can say what you want about my dad, but don't you dare talk about my mama!

My mom never left me. She did her best, obviously taking care of us. But she had her own issues. It wasn't easy for her by any means. But God told me, "You need to forgive your mother. When you were a little kid, you blamed your mother for choosing your stepfather over you."

Even though he would threaten to kill her if she left, I didn't understand that as a kid. I just didn't know how to process it. Every time we would try to get away from him, she would always end up going back.

He would find us, we would escape, and he would find us again. It was always frightening whenever he would show up at the house. It was so scary as a child and even as a teenager. He was a large, imposing man too. He was 6'1", 220 pounds, with zero fat, twenty-inch arms, and had been in the Marine Corps. He used to burn cigarettes on his arms and he carried guns all the time. That's probably why I wasn't afraid of anybody when I was older because I had to deal with that growing up.

The Lord said, "You need to forgive her." I couldn't believe it. This is where many people get stuck; there are people you must forgive that you may not even know you need to forgive, even from childhood. The Lord was telling me to forgive her because it was affecting my current status. So, I forgave my mom. Then I forgave all the other people who hurt me. I even had to forgive myself. Forgiveness was a battle that I had to fight to be healthy and whole.

After forgiving everyone I could think of, I left the prayer room, went to bed, and slept like a baby. It was the best sleep I had ever had in my life. I woke up the next day, and everything I saw looked like Candy Land, the children's game. It was like that for three days straight. Thank God I was new in the home, so I didn't have much responsibility.

For three days in a row, I was basically non-functional. I was in the Spirit realm.

What I experienced in those three days was amazing; the trees were praising God, I could hear birds singing for the first time in my life, and they were worshiping God. I saw everything with new eyes, and the colors were so vivid. I remember this was when I realized I was colorblind. Normal for me was seeing everything in different shades of gray. But now, everything was not only in color but a vivid color like Dorothy in the Land of Oz.

Then, after about the third day, it started to fade off me, like waking up from a dream. As cool as the last three days had been, I knew I couldn't live my life like that. But from that day on, I never blanked out and got angry like that ever again. I never fought the way I used to in my life anymore. Forgiveness had caused that spirit of anger to leave my life for good.

6

I Know What It's Like

I'm so thankful for every one of these stories from my life. No matter how crazy or difficult, funny or sad they may be, they have become part of what God has used to make me into the man I am today. I'm thankful because, like bricks in a building, God used every single one of those experiences to build my life. I'm the pastor I am today because of those life experiences. So I'm genuinely thankful for them.

I'm grateful because it's my stories that allow me to feel the pain of others. I hear their cries because I know what it's like to be abused, abandoned, and left fatherless. I know what it's like to be poor; I grew up surrounded by poverty and lack. Because I've lived the life I've lived, I know what it's like to be told you're stupid and ugly, and you'll never make it. I was told those things every single day of my life growing up.

Because I've been in prison, I know what it's like to be in bondage, to have my freedom stripped away from me, and to lay in bed every night afraid for my life. I know what it's like to want to kill myself and feel that unrelenting desperation. I know what it's like not to have any hope or to feel the little hope I did have turn to anger and rage, hardening myself so no one would ever hurt me again. I know what it's like to hurt so badly that I made the declaration, from that time forward, I would be the one hurting other people. I know what that kind of demon possession feels like.

Every day I get out of bed with the full knowledge there are people right now in my city and around the world who are hurting. They're crying out and if I just sit back and do nothing, these poor people could die in their loneliness, bondage, despair, pain, and sin. But, when I close my eyes, I can see their faces, which drives me forward every single day.

So, yes, I thank God for these stories because they have become part of the fabric of God's plan for my life.

MY ROLE MODELS

I've always thought there are probably two people in the Bible I identify with the most, but now, as I write, I can think of a third and even a fourth person from scripture. The first is Paul because I've certainly felt like him before in my life. Like Paul, God knocked me off my horse, landing me flat on the ground. Remember, God told Paul, "You kick against the goads" (Acts 26:14). Basically, God is telling Paul, "This is your last chance, buddy. If you don't serve me, you're a dead man." Sometimes you need an ultimatum like that when God knocks you off your horse! That's what happened to me. He knocked me down and said, "You're doing all this destruction in the city. You're messing up all these people's lives. Your time is up, buddy. Enough is enough. Either you're going to serve me, or you're done." And that's why I relate to

Paul so well. He was much worse than a murderer. He was almost like a serial killer or an assassin. And yet God forgave him and not only forgave him but powerfully used him. When I first got saved, Paul's revelation was like my revelation—the renewing of my mind was complete, just like Paul's was. He got a fresh, second chance to answer the call of God.

When I get to heaven, I want to sit down for a long conversation with Paul and another person I identify with, David. I just love King David! I connect with who King David was in scripture because of his passionate love for God. my journey of intimacy with God, knowing God, and being close to Him reminds me so much of David's journey. I want to be as close to God as David was. He was raised from obscurity simply because he was a man after God's own heart.

The third person from scripture I identify with, who is probably the one I connect with the most, is Moses. He murdered a man in Egypt and then ran for his life to the wilderness. And yet, through a burning bush, God called Moses from the backside of the desert to return to Egypt and boldly stand before Pharaoh and declare, "Let my people go! Set them free from their bondage and slavery. Let them go!" That's my calling, to stand up to our enemy, the devil, the "pharaoh" of this world, and boldly declare, "Let my people go!" I've learned a lot through the example that Moses set. The Bible says that he was the humblest man on the Earth, and yet he was one of the most powerfully used.

The fourth person I identify with is Moses' second in command, Joshua, who served Moses well and was a coura- geous warrior. God called him to take back the Promised

Land, taking a nation of slaves and turning them into a nation of warriors to battle against God's enemies. Now that's a calling I can identify with!

"God has a plan for your life." When I first heard that, in my mind, I thought, *Yeah, a plan to hurt me; a plan to curse me.* That's because I felt like a hurt, cursed young man. But then the truth dawned on me. I realized, *Wait a minute, if God could use guys like Paul or David or Moses or Joshua, even after all the terrible things they did, then maybe He can use me too.*

That's when God gave me the verse Jeremiah 29:11 (NIV), "'For I know the plans I have for you,'" declares the Lord, "'plans to prosper you and not to harm you, plans to give you hope and a future.'" After reading that, I told God, "Whatever you want me to do, wherever you want me to go, whatever it is you need from me, I'm yours, all of me." I've tried to live like that for the last thirty years.

A LESSON IN BROKENNESS

One of the major strongholds in my life used to be pride, which is a little surprising to me today, looking back on it, considering it came out of being rejected and feeling insecure. Back then, nobody could tell me what to do or when to do it. So God had to break that pride and teach me how to submit to leadership. It's interesting because God put me under several Christian leaders who were so carnal you'd never know they were Christians. They didn't like anyone, and not surprisingly, none of them are serving

God today. But God used those guys to rub me the wrong way on purpose to reveal the pride in my heart.

God took me through a couple of years of bad bosses like them in order to renew my mind. God was preparing me for what He would use me for in the future, and He knew there was no place for pride in that future. He was forging my character in the flames of frustration by having me put up with such terrible leaders. He used each of these men to teach me, even though most of them weren't right with God at all. I knew that, yet they would always do stuff to me, trying to offend me.

But God taught me how to respond out of humility instead of pride, "Go up to them and apologize. Tell them you're sorry even if you've done nothing to offend them," knowing full well I was not wrong. But I learned that it was not about them, and it was not about who was right or who was wrong. It was about God breaking that pride in me. When I would tell them, "I'm sorry if I've done anything to offend you," they would respond with a haughty, prideful look, making me want to haul off and slug somebody. It was never-ending.

For example, while living at the home, I started working for a Christian, but again, he was an evil Christian boss. He was just so nitpicky and mean. I would get very angry; One time, I remember almost wanting to hit him with a weed whacker! But that spirit of anger was gone, so I didn't do it, but I could feel that old familiar feeling start to rise up. I had conquered it, so it didn't, but that's how mad I was getting. Sometimes I'd be so miserable that I'd cry all the way home after work. I'd cry out, "God, why?" and God would just say, "I know it's hard, mijo. But humble yourself. Seek the lowest place. Tell him you're sorry for everything that's gone wrong." I'm like, "Wow, God . . . are you sure about that?" God loved me enough to break my pride.

Then there was another boss, a construction supervisor, a notoriously mean guy. This guy wasn't even a Christian. He was just mean. So, again, whenever he would yell at me, God had me respond by telling him, "I'm sorry if I did anything wrong or anything to offend you."

After that, I had another boss, a Christian contractor. He was a big, tall man, like my stepfather. He was very imposing. He would just put me down and make me feel stupid. Again, I'd get angry. One time I got so mad I almost hit him with a shovel! But God said, "That's what we're going to deal with, that pride right there; that can't go where I'm sending you." Remember, humility will keep you open and sensitive to the word of the Lord.

The lesson of humility is so important for us to learn in our lives as Christians. We must carry humility as a critical ingredient of our character. The key to our humility is brokenness. Contentment comes from our brokenness, being grateful, and never forgetting the "Egypt" that God has brought us out of. I think that was a big lesson God had to teach me. My pastor would always remind me, even to this day, "Stay humble, young man." He dealt with a lot of drug addicts and messed up people just like I was. He told me, "You were so messed up when I saw you. I'm just going to be honest, I didn't think you were going to make it. But, every time I would preach, you would be the one down front at the altar.

People would be leaving the church, and you would still be there, on your face at the altar. Then after a while, I thought, maybe God's going to do something with this kid."

Little by little, my pastor began to see what God was doing in my life and he would continue to drill humbleness into me. To this day, I strive for humility in my life. Not fake, "religious" humility, but a sincere attitude of gratitude that has served me well through the years. I have to remember to stay humble and broken before the Lord with all that God has given me because I don't ever want to go through that kind of humiliation again; I'd rather just humble myself. The scripture says, "You either fall on the rock, or the rock falls on you" (Matthew 21:44). I decided years ago that I was going to humble myself, and I realized the quickest way I could do that was to stay grateful and thankful.

THE STRONGHOLD OF OFFENSE

According to Mark 4, the enemy comes to steal the Word soon after it's been sown in our hearts. One of the ways he steals the Word is through offense. Offense is resentment that someone *chooses* because they feel they've been insulted in some way; it's part of our carnal nature. Notice I said, "chooses." Offense isn't something that just happens to people; they must choose whether to be offended or not.

Some people, like me, were raised to be easily offended. Offense was all around me growing up. I thought it was the standard response whenever I felt like I had been wronged in some way. I didn't realize at the time that this was another dangerous stronghold keeping me from being all God created me to be. This stronghold was blocking me from fulfilling my calling of going into a lifetime of ministry. God knew that this stronghold would have to be pulled down too if I was going to succeed. He knew that there's always an opportunity for offense when you're in the ministry. This was something that God had to deal with in me before He could trust me with more influence. He wanted to deal with the root of bitterness that had grown deep in my heart from all those years of choosing offense.

God was humbling me and teaching me how to win over offense because He knew I couldn't carry offense into the places He wanted me to go. He knew that I'd be leading thousands of leaders worldwide and teaching them how to lead thousands of people. Offense was a luxury I could no longer afford. It's one of the main areas the devil uses to knock people out of the race. For this reason, God took me to an extreme in this area, giving me all those terrible bosses. He taught me how to deal humbly with difficult people instead of choosing to get offended. Today I train our young people in this same process. I've learned that even the marriage relationship will be easier than you think if you learn to beat this thing; it's all about humility.

In my church, we have zero tolerance for offense. It's a "no offense" zone, a "no strife" zone. If you're offended, you'll have to let it go. Even Jesus said that if your brother owes you, it's better to take the hit and eat the debt for the sake of peace and to trust God to avenge you. That was my issue. I always felt like I had to avenge myself. But God says, "No, I'm your avenger now. I'm your exceedingly great reward. I'm your defender. I'm your protector. I'm your father now. Trust me." It takes a long time sometimes, but eventually, you learn to trust God.

All those people who were offending me while I was still growing and maturing in the Lord, I eventually realized it was never about them. It was about me choosing God instead of offense. God knew my offense wasn't going to change anything. All those bosses were still going to be just as mean whether I was offended or not.

This is funny because every boss I had for years was the same; they were all mean and harsh. I prayed every day that God would give me another job. Then I'd get a new job, and it would be the same thing, an evil boss. This tendency continued to follow me until finally, at my last position, God said, "Okay, you've learned this lesson; humility has been built into your heart." This is the brokenness I am talking about. Like my pastor reminded me, we must stay broken before the Lord.

I learned that you could either humble yourself or wait until God has to humble you. I was humbled by God before, and I didn't like it very much! It's much better to choose to live in humility, genuine humility. I keep myself broken now because I never want to forget the house of bondage I came out of. I don't choose to remember it because of the pain; I remember it in a grateful way because of the many lessons I learned there.

HUMILITY, YOUR SECRET WEAPON

I learned that brokenness is the secret behind spiritual warfare. I had brokenness when I had nothing else. I had no faith yet. I didn't know the Word of God yet. I didn't know how to operate in the gifts of the Spirit yet. But I was broken; I had humility. Brokenness, thanksgiving, and praise are the most powerful spiritual weapons you can have in your arsenal. The devil has no answer against those kinds of weapons.

I tell young Christians, "You may not know the Bible yet. You may not have just the right scripture for the moment, but thank God for saving you and for all He's done in your life. You may not be where you want to be but thank God you're not where you used to be!" That alone will break all warfare off of you and put the enemy back in his place. That's how Paul broke free from prison. He and Silas just praised God. They thanked God. They were worshiping the Lord when He came with power, shook the prison walls, and set them free.

That kind of gratitude lifts us from depression and sets us free from bondage. I used to struggle with that kind of mental depression. Because of how methamphetamine affected me, I would be all over the place emotionally. Brokenness and praise were two of the ways I could break that feeling before I learned how to use the Word. After that, I stabilized myself through praise, thanksgiving, worship, and the Word. That's probably one of the reasons why I'm so close to God today. I finally learned that the closer I got to Him, the better I felt.

I Know What It's Like

When you choose to live with that kind of perspective, with an attitude of gratitude, there's no such thing as a bad day. When the devil comes against you, telling you, "Your prayers aren't working. God can't hear you. He has abandoned you." You could start feeling sorry for yourself, thinking, *God, I'm here serving you, and I'm here all by myself.* But brokenness and praise have the power to break up that pity party if you never forget where you've come from. You are assured that God listens and that He hears you. You remember that He gives grace to the humble and provides humility and power to the weak. Never forget where you come from! Be grateful for everything that God has given you!

7

Hide and Seek

"One thing I have desired of the Lord, that will I seek after; that I may dwell in the house of the Lord all the days of my life, to behold the beauty of the Lord, and to enquire in his temple. For in the time of trouble he shall hide me in his pavilion: in the secret of his tabernacle shall he hide me; he shall set me up upon a rock" (Psalms 27:4-5 KJV).

PRESSING INTO THE LORD

An interesting thing happened to me as all of that pride and offense began to break off. God put an insatiable appetite for Him inside of me. I found myself wanting to know Him more, immerse myself more in His presence, and continually feast on God's Word.

With my whole being, I began pressing into God while I was still living in the home. So many other guys in the home would just be hanging out and talking. Meanwhile, I'd try to find a quiet place to read, pray, and press into God. Unfortunately, my whole prayer life revolved around the timetables of a bunch of men. The lack of privacy was tough on me. I wanted to have my own place where God and I could be together. That was my prayer and all I really wanted in those days.

Finally, God blessed me with a little place that contained a twin bed, a small desk, and a dresser; that was about all you could fit in the space. It was right behind my pastor's home, and I was so happy for that answer to prayer. It was a tiny space, but it was all mine. I lived there for around four years, and that's where I learned to pray. Looking back, I can see that those years were really a time of consecration for me.

Left:

Jason at his wedding with his sister and brother.

Right:

Jason Lozano, twenty-years-old in Bible college at the men's home.

That little place is where I began to press into God. I worked just enough to make what I needed to pay for Bible college and rent, the rest of my time was spent with God. I was constantly at the church on the altar. I would pray all night many times, always spending time with God. That was my whole world during those years.

I had to ride my bike for a good hour to get to Bible college. Before I could afford the bike, it was a bus ride that would get me there or I sometimes had to walk, even if it was raining. That's just how badly I wanted to do well in school. I was willing to do whatever it took to succeed. Believe me, it was tough, and I had a lot to overcome. God even had to reteach me how to properly read and write. It was almost like learning a new language, because of the life I'd led before coming to the Lord.

One minister who helped me in those early days was Bishop T.D. Jakes. He talked about the process God takes people through to raise them up and pull them out of their pain. His whole message was on healing the brokenhearted and I could identify because that's what God was doing in me. Bishop Jakes' messages imparted the healing of the brokenhearted to me and were very inspirational, motivational, and just what I needed.

As much as I was pressing into the Lord, the enemy had really stepped up his attacks on me, trying hard to steal the Word. The devil would try to lie to me when I walked to school. There were times when I was walking in the rain, and other kids were passing by, driving nice cars. They were good kids, and we were the same age, but the devil would tell me, "You don't belong here. You're too stupid to go to this school. Look, everyone else is driving, and you're over here walking in the rain. You're an idiot, and you can't even read."

Every time I'd sit down to do an assignment, I had to have a dictionary open on the desk because I couldn't read. I had a hard time because I was learning so slowly. I had to have a dictionary just to be able to read my books. I'd sit in class, and the enemy would lie to me, saying, "Just run out of here, you don't belong here, you're stupid, what are you doing here?" I'd have to fight that negativity every day for a long time. But I just continued to go to class and press into God. Even on lunch breaks when everyone else was going out to eat, I went to the chapel and spent time with God.

The enemy's attacks were a daily thing. So I had to make a constant decision, saying, "No, I'm not going to do that. Instead, I'm going to seek God. I'm going to press into God." During that time, I began to research the scriptures, diving into the Word of God, doing everything I knew to do to get a hold of Him, and seeking Him in prayer.

Money didn't even appeal to me anymore. The more I pressed into God, the more those worldly desires fell by the wayside. The enemy tried to tempt me, telling me about all the stuff I didn't have, things I could no longer afford. But his schemes didn't work on me because I felt like I had everything I could ever want.

Then one day, I came home, and God had touched a brother's heart to give me a bike. There it was, a beautiful bike in the living room just waiting for me. At that moment, that was the greatest miracle I'd ever had. I mean, the way God prospered me in those days was amazing.

A LESSON IN CONTENTMENT

I remember when I was living at the home, we would go to church camp at Silverwood Lake every summer. Silverwood Lake is a beautiful spot up in the mountains northeast of L.A. It was a great place to escape the stress of the city, a quiet place where people could really do business with God. And it was the place that I preached my very first sermon outside of the recovery home.

One day my pastor approached me and said, "Tonight, I want you to share the Bible study." I was so scared, thinking, *Oh man, what am I going to say?* It was one thing for me to get up in front of a couple of dozen guys at the home, but this was much different. I would be speaking to a couple hundred families! I remember looking at their boats, RVs, and gear, and thinking, *What do I have to share? I have nothing. I have no money. I have no car. I have nothing. Why would he pick me to share?* That's when God told me, "I want you to preach because you have something more than they have. You have contentment. You have satisfaction. I want you to teach them the secret of being content."

That was a secret that the Apostle Paul knew. He said, "I can have a lot or nothing, but I've learned the secret of being content" (Philippians 4:12). That secret is a powerful weapon in spiritual warfare because the enemy likes to press us about all the things we don't have. The devil can't fight you there anymore because you can now beat those attacks with humility, gratefulness, and the secret of contentment. That is the secret Paul had that caused him to conquer in so much warfare.

A LESSON ON THE AUTHORITY OF GOD

I had several supernatural experiences in those early days. God was teaching me so much. I had a lot to learn! One of the most powerful lessons I learned was about God's authority and power. I was at the American Bible Institute, now the Latin American Bible College. I was in the school, and my friend, the one who spoke those words over me and I slugged in the head—we are friends now—he ended up turning his life around and started attending the same Bible school as me.

Eventually, the school hired my friend to be on staff, and they were able to give him a little studio apartment on campus as a part of his compensation. He would let me use it during the day from time to time while he was at work and I wasn't in class. So one day I was in the studio watching TV, just wearing my boxers and tank top, lying on the bed, relaxing.

What happened next was so weird. I don't know how to explain it to this day. The bathroom door was right next to the bed where I was laying. It flew open suddenly, like King Kong had kicked it. I looked over and saw the biggest, meanest demon; he looked like Shaquille O'Neal but five times bigger and buffed out. He looked like a bull with ugly, yellow, angry eyes and he came straight toward me.

Hide and Seek

The colossal demon jumped on me and started choking me to death. I couldn't breathe; I couldn't talk, and was thinking, *What in the heck am I going to do?* Then out of my spirit came the name, "Jesus." When I said the name out loud, "Jesus," I could see that the demon was afraid. Because I've been in the streets and been around fear, I recognized that same fear in those big, ugly, yellow eyes. I realized, *Oh you don't like that do you?* So, I said the name a little bit louder, and when I said it, it was like something hit him with a baseball bat. He began to loosen his grip on my throat. Then I said it louder, and he let go even more. Finally, I shouted "JESUS!" and ran him right out of that house.

When I went outside, I realized the door had closed behind me. I was locked out! There I was, out on the front porch screaming, "Jesus!" with my boxers on, in the middle of the college campus! Quickly, I used my past B&E (breaking-and-entering) skills and broke back into the studio through the back window. I jumped back in and opened up all the windows and doors. I fell back on the bed, exhausted, wondering, *What in the heck just happened?*

The devil doesn't try that kind of stuff with me anymore because I know better now. He was just trying to take advantage of me, to intimidate me. That's how desperate he got because I was just learning about my authority back then. But today I know the power and authority that's found in the name of Jesus.

Okay, now let me tell you the Church's Chicken story.

CHURCH'S CHICKEN

Back in those days, about the only place we could afford to eat out was Church's Chicken, so we ate there a lot! You could get a whole meal for like $2. Anyway, I had a friend from church who had gotten into hairdressing. The problem was, he was using his job as a way to meet women. I knew all about his fooling around, but we remained friends. I was trying to talk to him about not compromising his walk with God and we ended up going to Church's Chicken on a Friday night for dinner. We were at the table talking and I told him, "You can't be playing around with sin. You know that messing around with those girls is wrong." The next thing I knew, I was starting to move in the gifts of the Spirit. I was sitting there talking and a couple came and sat at the table behind us. Suddenly, I heard the Lord say, "Pray for them," and then I heard the word "adultery" come up in my spirit.

Now in the restaurant at the time me and my friend were the only customers, then the couple came in and sat behind us, and a couple of church ladies from an African American church sat at another table. Next to the register, there was a guy with a turban, and there was also a lady working the drive-thru.

I leaned in and whispered to my friend, "Hold on. I have to pray for this couple real quick. I feel like I need to go pray for them." I got up, turned around, and said, "How are you doing? Can I pray for you?" They said, "Yeah, sure." So, I stretched my hands out to pray for them. The next thing I knew, I was prophesying the word of the Lord. I told the lady what God was telling me about her and what God was saying to him. Basically, they were both living in adultery. He was a backslidden minister. They needed to get their lives right with God. They both broke down and started crying when the power of God hit them. It was pretty crazy, but that's not even the craziest part.

I call it the *Twilight Zone*, and it had never happened to me before and it's never happened to me since. I looked over and the church ladies were eating their chicken, then abruptly they stopped moving, just like in a *Twilight Zone* episode. I looked over at the register guy in the turban and he wasn't moving either. Everyone in the restaurant was frozen, not moving at all! The person buying food at the drive-thru window wasn't even moving. Everyone was standing as still as statues. Meanwhile, my friend was wide awake watching it all.

I was moving in a powerful anointing with this couple. They told me that they would stop committing adultery, get right with God, and get back in ministry. It was a crazy event. Afterward I looked at my friend, and he was floored. So I said, "Let's go. Obviously, there's no more reasons for us to eat here." Then we got in the car, and I looked at my friend and said, "Yeah, you better stop playing around with those girls!"

In the moment, I acted as if things like that happened to me all the time, even though it had never happened to me before or since. Of course, my friend was significantly impacted that day, but these are the kind of experiences in those early years that God was giving me. I don't know how or why He did it like that, but He did. Kenneth Hagin helped me understand this a bit. He said that there were times that Jesus would visit him and talk to him for like an hour and a half each time. But he said the Lord stopped doing that with him after a season.

It's like God sometimes does things like that just for a season. I didn't understand it for a long time, but those experiences anchored me in what I do now. They molded me and marked me. So, when it comes to the gifts of the Spirit and the authority of God, the Spirit realm, and the power of God, I have never forgotten these things, and I never will.

AN OUT-OF-BODY EXPERIENCE

My pastor at the home let a Spanish church use our church building. They had a pastor there who was known as a prophet. This guy was really powerful. He was one of those guys who was very accurate in his prophecies. So I'd go to their Spanish services, even though I didn't speak the language.

This Spanish church would have three- or four-hour-long services. I wasn't used to that; our services were much shorter. Even though there weren't many people attending the services, the services were mighty. I liked them because of the powerful anointing the pastor was carrying.

I was so hungry for God. I wanted everything He wanted to give me, so I would wait until the end of the service and then go up front for prayer from the pastor. I didn't really understand what was said since it was in Spanish, but I liked the prayer part. When the pastor started to pray for people, including me, it was like dynamite went off inside me. **BOOM!** I was on my back.

It's hard to explain but it was like my spirit came halfway out of my body. I looked to my right, and other people were laid out on the floor. I looked to my left, and the same thing, people laid out on the floor. My flesh, my body, was on the floor, looking up at my spirit. And what I saw was my spirit looked like platinum. Have you ever seen a black gold ring? Like platinum, that's how it looked. I'm big in spirit, so I always tell people now as a joke, "I'm bigger than you think!" (I'm really just 5'5".) But I know what my spirit looks like now.

MY SISTER GETS A MIRACLE

If you have these kinds of experiences, they are things you never forget. For example, I have a sister named Tamar who used to be a prodigal daughter. Today she's serving God as a children's pastor. God has turned everything around for her.

Several years ago, when my sister had my niece in the hospital, they had to do a C-section. My precious niece Hannah was born without a problem. She was fine. But later, my sister began to develop some complications. They didn't know what was wrong with her, so the doctors operated on her again. They closed her up when they assumed they had fixed the problem. But while in recovery, it became obvious that something still wasn't right. My sister started turning blue. She was not getting enough oxygen, and she was dying. That's when everyone started getting extremely nervous because her life was on the line.

As the doctors operated on her again, my mom got every-one into a prayer chain. We all started praying and believing God for healing. While all this was happening, I was at my job. When I was finally able to get away, I raced toward the hospital. The next thing I knew, I had this crazy open vision.

I wasn't expecting this. I wasn't believing for this. It just came on me suddenly, out of the blue. One minute I'm driving to the hospital on Whittier Blvd. in Los Angeles; the next minute, I have an open vision. I'm no longer driving, I'm up on top of the car. Then, in an instant, I was in the hospital, looking down at my sister, who was on the operating table.

As I hovered in the room over my sister, I saw a little monkey-looking demon sitting on my sister's stomach. The demon was about three feet tall and looked like an alien with a medical mask on. It was wearing little medical glasses and a little medical cap on its head; its fingers and toes were razors like Edward Scissorhands.

I knew all this by intuition. He was cutting up my sister, cutting up her stomach. That little demon knew exactly what he was doing. Surrounding my sister were four big giant demons, like the one I saw in the Bible school that I talked about earlier. They were guardians and their assignment was to protect the smaller demon doing all the damage. He was doing the work, and they were protecting him. This was straight-up spiritual warfare. This was the real deal.

The next thing I knew, breaking out of the ceiling came the biggest, baddest angel I'd ever seen. The enormous creature was blackened like he'd been in battle. He wasn't weakened, he was blackened by battle smoke.

Almost as if he were in a battle, he darted out of the ceiling, and like an eagle snatching a trout, the angel grabbed that little demon and squeezed it. I heard a crack, and that demon was dead. The angel yanked it off my sister and took it straight up and it was gone. The four demons that were still there looked stupidly at one another. They knew they had blown it. The devil had commissioned them, and now they had to go back and describe what had happened on their watch, like soldiers reporting to the commanding officer.

Suddenly, I was back in my car, driving to the hospital, but now I was confident in my spirit that the crisis was over, and that my sister had been healed. When I arrived at the hospital, my mom came running out to meet me. She cried, "Mijo, you're not going to believe it!" I smiled and said, "I know mom, Tamar's fine, isn't she?" My mom said, "How did you know?" I said, "Mom, you're not going to believe this. Sit down and let me tell you what I just saw!"

My sister was miraculously healed that day. She was fine. She lived, didn't die, and now she's serving God. That's the authority we take in the spirit realm. All of our prayers that day broke the demonic strategy against my sister. We had assumed that it was a medical issue, and it was, but in reality, it was a spiritual issue. The spiritual principle here is: Once you break something in the spiritual world, the miracle shows up in the natural world.

Scripture says that "Whatever we bind on earth will be bound in heaven, and whatever we loose on earth will be loosed in heaven" (Matthew 18:18). The authority of the name of Jesus is that at the sound of that name, demons tremble, just at the mention of that name, they must flee. It's a name "far above every other name" (Philippians 2:9).

The spirit realm is real; the authority we carry is also real. The power we have in Him is no joke. I always tell the church that sometimes there are things in our lives that are there illegally. We're waiting on God to take authority, but God is waiting on us. So, if you want to be free, you must learn to walk in that authority.

8

A Call to Pastor

When I consider where I am today and what I'm doing right now, I easily get overwhelmed with emotion. It is nothing short of a miracle from God. Looking back, I can see times in my life, many times, when God stepped in and spared my life. I can see instances where the Holy Spirit gently guided me in the right direction, even though I had no idea at the time what He was doing.

A few chapters back, I told you about the time I was called up on stage in the middle of a service and received a call into the ministry. By the time I left the home, I had become a traveling evangelist, and I enjoyed it. I was ministering and going to college, working on my degree in psychology. My goal was just to be in ministry with no thought of ever having a church of my own. I didn't want to be a pastor. I was enjoying my life, traveling, and speaking to various groups, in many different places. It was hard for me to imagine being tied down to just one place and ministering to just one group of people.

If I'm honest with myself, I didn't want to pastor mostly because of the fear of rejection. I had seen everything my pastor had gone through, helping people, and then watching those same people turn around and leave the church or spread untrue, hurtful rumors about him. But, today, I understand that it's just the nature of pastoring; it can be quite violent on the soul.

So, I steered away from pastoring. I thought that, for me, being an evangelist was a much better fit. I was able to simply come and go out of places, finding that a much safer way for me to be in ministry. However, twenty years ago, my spirit was not settled. I realized something was off and not quite right.

I sought the Lord for a few days, fasting and pressing in. Finally, I asked the Lord, "God, what are you saying to me? What's wrong? I know something isn't right." Then, I had an encounter with God. He spoke to me, and the message was so clear. He said, "I've heard the cries of the people and I'm sending you to the pharaohs of Whittier/Los Angeles, California to declare, 'Let my people go!'" Several miracles happened to me at that moment.

GOD'S BURDEN

The first miracle was that God put the burden of the people on me, what I call "God's burden." Those words, *I've heard the cries of the people,* weighed so heavily on me that I thought they'd crush me. When that burden hit me, it changed my life. After that moment I couldn't do anything other than pastor. There was no way on earth I could do anything else. Passion for that burden overrode any fears I might have had about being a pastor. Overwhelming compassion and a newfound, heartbreaking love overrode the fear of rejection and the fear of being hurt. Then the vision came: "Let my people go that they may worship." Then God began to deal with me on all the pharaohs I was going to have to conquer.

Immediately, I felt the weight of the new calling to pastor, but I had some concerns about returning to Whittier. Years before, when I left the city of Whittier to move into the home, organized crime had put a hit on my life to kill me. Remember, before serving God, I was a drug dealer, and of course I upset a lot of people. After the men's home, I had served God for about nine years but now God was calling me back.

I asked Him, "Lord, do you want me to die for you? Is that what you're asking?" Because at that moment, I was willing. And He said, "No. All the people who are after your life are dead." When I took a moment to think about it, it was true; everyone in Whittier who wanted me dead had died. God didn't kill these people; their lifestyle did. The Bible says that "if you live by the sword, you die by the sword" (Matthew 26:52), so their lifestyle did that to them. They were all dead and gone.

Then God told me one of the pharaohs He was sending me to confront was the pharaoh of religion, which was a shock to me at first. It's fascinating because the pharaoh of religion is stronger than the pharaohs of addiction, poverty, or brokenness. Organized religion is just man's attempt to reach God on his own. Religion embraces the trappings of godliness but denies it's true power, removing all spiritual authority.

STARTING BY FAITH

So, I called my pastor and said, "Pastor, I need to talk to you right away. Let's have breakfast tomorrow. I just had an encounter with God, and I need to talk it through." In the ten years of our relationship, I never told him that something like this had happened to me. He said, "Yeah, we need to talk." So, we were sitting there, having breakfast, and I told him what had happened to me. He knew immediately that it was God. He told me, "Right, you never wanted to pastor before. I've been trying to get you to pastor forever, and you wouldn't do it, so that message has to be from God."

I told him, "I need to start this church in Whittier. It's something I've got to do just as soon as possible." He said, "Okay, when do you want to start it?" I said, "This Sunday!" He looked at me like, *Are you sure*? He asked, "Who are you going to use to help you?" I told him, "Well, I have my ministry staff. I have four people on staff and three more people I reached through our evangelistic ministry. With those seven, I figure we'll go ahead and answer the call and start the church."

I started the church with those seven people—four of them from my ministry staff and three guys who were barely sober. My musician was a very smart guy, but he was addicted to drugs, and would sometimes disappear on Saturday nights. Sunday morning would come, and he'd be missing, and we would have to go and look for him. I'd find him and bring him out, pray for him, and he would play for worship. I didn't schedule the church service to begin at the normal time because I knew there was no way the people I was trying to reach would come to church at 10 a.m., so I started the service at two o'clock in the afternoon.

I went to the nightclubs and bars in the area and witnessed to the people I found there. I told them about my new church and invited them to come visit on Sunday at two o'clock. I encouraged them, "If you're hungover, don't worry about it. We'll give you a bowl of soup and an Advil!" It didn't matter to me; I wanted to get them to church. I wasn't looking for people who had their act together, on the contrary, I was looking for *lost* people whose lives were in chaos.

Eventually people came, and they started getting saved. These were very humble beginnings. The building we found to meet in was tiny, only holding about twenty people. All I could afford at the time were twenty ugly pink chairs purchased on surplus liquidation. They only cost us about $4 a chair, so you can imagine how bad those chairs were. We had to borrow the sound system; we had to borrow everything in those early days! We started the church by faith, and God was with us.

A LIMITED MENTALITY

What God has done with our church since those days has truly been a miracle. But one of the things that I had to learn to conquer in this process was a limited mentality. In Exodus 3:11, God said to Moses, "I need you to do this." Moses responded, "Who am I, that I should bring the children of Israel out of Egypt?" The Bible says, "Be not conformed to this world but be transformed by the renewing of your mind" (Romans 12:2 ESV).

Satan does all he can to conform us to a limited mentality. He starts his attacks early on in our lives; he uses broken homes and different types of abuses, addictions, and negative mindsets in our home environments to create these destructive forms of thinking. These negative thoughts become a belief system. These belief systems become our character, and our character defines our destiny.

For me, this negative belief system, brought about by the scheming of Satan, severely limited my thinking to believing that I could never do anything great for God, that there was no way I could ever do something as bold and courageous as taking the city for God. In fact, in Numbers 13:33, when the spies were asked to scout out the Promised Land, they came back and told Moses and the people, "We can't do it. There are giants in the land, and we are like grasshoppers in their eyes." This kind of limited thinking, these mental strongholds, causes us to live beneath our potential. I want to make a heavy statement that the Lord taught me; He said, "What you're dealing with is what the Israelites dealt with."

A limited mentality is the same tool used effectively by pharaoh and his taskmasters in Egypt. It's interesting if you study it because the brilliance of Egypt was in their taskmasters. They were able to build their kingdom on the backs of slaves. Even though the slaves outnumbered their masters and could have revolted at any time, they wouldn't do it because Pharaoh and his taskmasters had put them in bondage in their minds, along with their physical chains, for over four hundred years. As a result, the Israelites were defeated in their minds first.

The Egyptians would look for angry children with hot tempers who were more violent than other kids and develop them into their corps of taskmasters. They were well schooled in the art of intimidation, manipulation, and control. These taskmasters abused the Israelites for 430 years.

In the first and maybe second generations, I can imagine that the slaves probably tried to fight back against their taskmasters for how they were being treated. But by the time the third or fourth generations came around, the Egyptians probably didn't need taskmasters. By this time, the slave parents were talking to their children just like the harsh taskmasters, saying things like, "You can't do that! Don't you know we are slaves? We are impoverished, barely human."

That was exactly the limiting, negative mentality I had grown up with. This has become one of our church's primary messages. It's not just freedom from addiction or bondage. The real bondage is breaking the lid of limited thinking off people.

Once you learn to recognize it, you see it everywhere you look. For example, in Judges 6:17, Gideon asks, "How could I save Israel? My clan is the weakest in Manasseh. I'm the least in my father's house." That's limited thinking! Gideon's destiny was to be a valiant warrior, but the enemy was holding him back because of his negative mindset.

These limiting mentalities have stopped us from becoming all that God wants us to be, and I had to be willing to challenge that voice of Pharaoh. So, for the past twenty years, I have been ministering, doing spiritual warfare with just that kind of challenge, confronting Pharaoh to let my people go and set them free from bondage.

LIVING A LIFE WITHOUT LIMITS

This is why I love the Apostle Paul so much; he challenges us. He tells us to not be conformed to this world. To not be limited by our past experiences, or the things we've gone through. To not let the abuses or the voices of our past tell us we can't do something or that we're not able. That's become the life message for our church. We're learning that not only is God going to set you free from bondage, but He also wants you to live a life without limits; Living the life that God has predestined and preordained for you before Satan abused and lied to you and stole your true destiny.

Once you believe God, and have experienced a break-through, let Him heal your broken heart and set you free. What's next? Now you must begin to transcend. He set you free for a reason, for a purpose. He has a *plan* for your life!

That's where the word of faith has been such a tremendous blessing to me and this ministry. The word of faith helps you lift the lid on limited thinking and say, "I am the person God says I am. I'm going to choose to believe what God says, regardless of what my past says I am, or even what my mind says."

FEAR MUST GO!

I think conquering modern-day Pharaohs is where a lot of people are today in their spiritual journey. Religion will try to appease that. It'll say, "Hey, you know, you're doing better, you're doing okay now. You can take it easy and cruise for a while." But no, the Kingdom goes forward, it doesn't just coast. It continues to advance. To advance with it, the limited, negative mindsets all have to go: the fear of the giants, the fear of "we're not able," and the fear of "I can't." It all must go. God says we can, and "we can do all things through Christ, who strengthens us" (Philippians 4:13 NKJV).

Paul says, "I press on, that I may lay hold of the reason He laid hold of me" (Philippians 3:12). So why did God choose me? Some may say, "Oh, I was lost and found the Lord." But I tell the people in our church, "No, you did not 'find the Lord.' He found you! He was never lost; you were." He found you for a purpose and a reason. He's not intimidated by the abuse. He's not intimidated by your inability. He's not intimidated by your weaknesses. He's not intimidated by your sin. He knew who you were when He called you. Just like He knew who Gideon was, just like He knew who Moses was, just like He knew who Paul was.

That's the word that lifts the lid off limited thinking. Like He told Jeremiah, "Do not say, 'I am only a youth'" (1:17, RSV). Remember Jeremiah would say, "I'm too young. I don't have what it takes." Moses would say, "I'm a stutter." Gideon would say, "I'm the weakest in Manasseh." You find it over and over when God calls his servants. All of them feel like they're inadequate. But God says, "No, don't say you're that. Say what I say you are. And say what I tell you to say."

Paul says in 1 Corinthians 1:27, "God chooses the foolish things of this world to confound the wise." I looked up the word "foolish" in the original Greek and got the word "moronic," or the English word "moron." So, Paul is telling us in that verse that God looks for the biggest morons He can find, and He chooses them. Why does God choose the foolish? So, in the end, no one can get the glory but God. I'm not going to get the recognition for all these things God is doing, these thousands of souls being saved, and revival breaking out in L.A. In the end, it's God, it's all God.

OTHER PHARAOHS

God has us on assignment against other Pharaohs too. The pharaoh of poverty is high on our list because our church is big on prosperity, teaching people how to *own* the bricks instead of making the bricks. A big problem among folks in our community is a poverty mindset. Did you know that even people with plenty of money can have a poverty mindset? You can always tell because they're not generous. They don't know how to prosper. Their mindset is that of poverty, lack, and scarcity. They don't know how to walk in wisdom. The pharaohs of insecurity, intimidation, fear, rejection, where people don't even know how to be corrected anymore because they think correction is rejection, and the pharaoh of brokenheartedness. These are just some of the pharaohs we have to deal with most often.

Paul said, "I haven't arrived, but one thing I do know is I'm forgetting those things that are behind me, and reaching forward to what lies ahead of me" (Philippians 3:13). And that's a key, where Paul says, "I press toward the mark for the prize of the high call." That's one of the things I've walked in these thirty years, where there is a high call. I believe that pastoring this church is a high call.

I don't want to get to heaven and tell God that I didn't follow through on the high call because I was afraid. No, I want to get to heaven and have accomplished what I was supposed to accomplish, even through hardship. Like Paul said when he defended the call of God, "I was not disobedient to the heavenly vision, and the grace of God on my life was not in vain" (Acts 26:19). I want to stand before God one day and hear Him say, "Well done, my good and faithful servant."

It's love that breaks the spirit of Pharaoh in people's minds, both the love of people and the love of God. That's why the Bible says, "Perfect love casts out fear" (1 John 4:18). That includes the fear of failure, man, rejection, or any other fear you can imagine. That's one of the principles of the Word of God: setting us free. In Joshua 1:8, God tells young Joshua, "My destiny for your life is not connected to your sword or your battle strategy alone." He told Joshua, "It's connected to your obedience to meditate on my Word."

MEDITATE ON THE WORD

All those years I spent in that little room buried in the Word of God, consumed by it, all that time has paid a rich dividend. That's why some of the most valuable advice I can give any struggling believer is to meditate on God's Word.

Meditate on the Word, meditate on the Word. Spend time in the Word, spend time in the Word, spend time in the Word.

When you do that, the Word comes alive in you. Jeremiah said, "I wanted to be quiet. I didn't want to preach anymore." But he said, "His word was like a fire, and it was shut up in my bones, and I couldn't hold it back" (Jeremiah 20:9 KJ21). That right there is what brings freedom; that right there can shift people's lives. And if enough people are set free from bondage, lives are changed, and families are saved, that's how revival is released in our cities.

9

Healing the Brokenhearted

When I got saved, one of the first things I did was to look up the word "brokenhearted" in the dictionary. Reading that definition changed my life. It means something that's been "crushed, trampled on, broken into pieces, shattered, and smashed." Believe me; I know what it's like to suffer from a broken heart. I feel like much of my childhood was spent battling those feelings. I was crushed, trampled on, smashed, and shattered. By the time I became a teenager, I was a very broken young man.

I learned from my studies in psychology, and my understanding of the spiritual dynamics that take place when somebody has been broken, there's really no fixing them. There's no healing for that. My own experience bears this out. They can prescribe medication in an attempt to provide them with a little bit of a better life, but there's no real healing outside of God.

The Bible says God gives us an anointing that can heal a broken heart. God takes all the pieces of our lives, along with the brokenness and the devastation, and just like Humpty Dumpty, He puts us back together again. In the natural, there's no way that happens, you can't simply put somebody back together like they'd never been broken. But God has the power through His Holy Spirit, His anointing, and His Word to put us back together again, even better than before. And when we're raptured up to heaven, we will be completely whole.

That's one of the reasons I love God so much. Only He can restore and redeem what's been broken and crushed. I know that in my heart, from my own experience. He can put a broken, shattered life back together, and not just put it back together, but then He can make something beautiful out of it. God lovingly tells us, "Just because you went through a smashing or a shattering experience, you don't have to limit your life. Instead, I will take what you went through, turn it around, and use it for my glory. I didn't put you through it, but I can use it to make the devil pay back what he stole in your life."

FRUSTRATING THE ENEMY

I tell the church this all the time, "The enemy should've killed you when he had the chance! But it's too late now. He really messed up, letting you go." Imagine how frustrated the devil is with me. Just think about it . . . he took my dad, leaving me fatherless. He abused me every day through my stepdad. He did all that damage. He had me right where he wanted me. I was his soldier. He had me where I was being used by him heavily. He had me perfectly positioned to do even more terrible things for him. Then, right when the devil thought he had me for good, God came in and snatched me out of his grasp. Then God turned around and used me as a trophy for Him, sending me back to the very city where the devil had me in bondage. God redeemed me!

I mean, just imagine how frustrating that is for the enemy. He spent all those years working on me, getting me into bondage, only to have God come in and deliver me in a heartbeat. And not only does God deliver me, but He lifts that negative, victim mentality that the enemy worked so long to put on me. I know how the enemy thinks. I know his lies. I know what he tells people because I was in his world. I was his soldier. I know exactly what he's doing. I recognize his strategy, not just because I've read it in the Bible, but because I've lived it.

I know what he's doing to people, and my personal experience has become a mighty weapon in my hands against the schemes of the enemy, for me to be able to say, "No, no, no, I know what the enemy is doing. I know what he's trying to do here. I recognize that taskmaster, that Pharaoh of brokenheartedness, bondage, and limitation." People in that kind of bondage can't get free on their own no matter how badly they may want to.

SET FREE FROM BONDAGE

I remember I had so many different things I was in bondage to. I was addicted to crystal methamphetamine, and I was a bad drinker. But the drinking wasn't as bad as the methamphetamine was, and I would get high on meth all the time. I smoked speed every night and every day. Every night, I'd feel so guilty that I'd break my pipes and quit the drugs, vowing never to return. But the next day, I'd be back at it, doing drugs again. I couldn't get free no matter what I tried. I wanted to be free, but I just couldn't break the bondage.

That's when God spoke to me and said, "Mijo, enough is enough." His power hit me. He had the power to break that bondage and every other bondage that the enemy was using on me. God never sets you free just for the sake of freedom. God sets you free for a purpose, so eventually, you can set somebody else free. Freely you have received, freely you give.

MADE A BLESSING TO BE A BLESSING

That's one of my biggest challenges when ministering in the church world. I'll pray for people, and many times their response is, "Oh, I'm so blessed. I'm happy. I'm healed. I'm whole. I went through molestation, pain, and lack, and now God has healed and delivered me." But I always challenge them, "That's true, but now what are you going to do with it? You can't just be blessed. God says He gives you richly all things to enjoy. So, now you're enjoying it. But what are you going to do with your healing, your recovery, your break-through, your deliverance?"

Here's where we come into lifting the lid. God has set us free so that we can be a blessing to others. What are you going to do with the blessing God has given you? There is a young man in our church who God has delivered might-ily. He was a very burdened, broken young man who came out of our recovery home. But God put his broken life back together again and blessed him financially in a fantastic way.

Today, he's a multimillionaire who can help us fund many of our projects, giving huge amounts to the gospel, huge amounts. I'm humbled to say that many in our church are just like that young man.

That's what this powerful message does. It doesn't just say, "Okay, you're a drug addict, you're messed up, you're broken." This message blows the lid off brokenness and bondage. We routinely see people go from poverty and bondage to living life without limits. I believe that is why our church has been able to reach so many different types of people.

Whether you're broken into a million pieces or already blessed but want to take your life to another level, this message of freedom can meet you anywhere. It's not just a life of deliverance; It's also a life of purpose and greatness. And eventually, you get on the road to helping others. You've received your freedom now. What are you going to do with it? God blesses us so that we can be a blessing to others.

SAVED TO PLANT A SEED

But make no mistake, the enemy is always right there waiting to steal our blessing before we can pass it on to other people. I remember one time being asked to lead attendees in the offering at a minister's conference in the Big Bear Mountains outside L.A. The conference was being put on by Dr. A.L. Gill.

My wife, Liz, and I were excited. We'd decided to use the conference as an opportunity to sow a seed of faith into our TV ministry, believing God wanted to open that door for us. God told us He wanted us to give $5,000, which was a considerable amount for us in those days.

So, we're heading up into the mountains, on the way to Big Bear. In the car, it was me, Liz, and my son Joshua, who was just a toddler at the time. We were in the outside lane of a narrow two-lane highway. To my left was the inside lane but to my right was a sharp three-hundred-foot drop with no guardrail. I was "white-knuckle driving," knowing that if I went off the road there was no way we'd survive. To make matters worse, Joshua was in the back seat screaming because the altitude was hurting his ears.

I asked Liz to see if there was any way she could get him to calm down. So, just about the time she was getting ready to take her seatbelt off to attend to Joshua, the Lord spoke to her, "I can't protect you if you disobey the law of the land."

The next thing I know, an oncoming car jumped from his lane right into mine, speeding right at us, forcing me to swerve to my right . . . into midair and off the cliff. It was crazy. I've got to tell you; it was a miracle for sure. I don't know how long we were off the road in midair, but then, miraculously, we just jumped right back on the pavement, in our lane. That car passed by us harmlessly and kept going! We were saved!

Immediately Liz starts shouting, "Pull over! Pull over!" I shout back, "Honey, I can't pull over. I'm not even driving this car!" I finally calmed down a couple hundred yards later and pulled the car over. In a sudden gush of emotion, we both started crying, still trying to figure out what had just happened. One thing we were both absolutely sure about was it was a miracle!

We got to the conference and we sowed the seed that night during the offering that I led for the service. It was the largest one-time offering that Dr. Gill's ministry had ever received. It opened unbelievable doors to the nations for them, serving to expand their ministry exponentially.

After the conference, I realized that the devil didn't want us to sow that seed into the ministry. His plan was to keep us from the conference so we couldn't give that offering. He wanted to steal the seed. But God saved us and delivered us so that we could be a blessing to that ministry by the receiving of our offering.

DELIVERED FROM DEATH

In Chapter 7, I told you about preaching my first sermon. Well, there's more to that story. Remember, I was still living at the recovery home at this point. We were headed up to Silverwood Lake and on the freeway in the ministry van. There was no guardrail in the middle, separating the north and southbound lanes. There was just this huge dirt road, about the width of five freeway lanes.

We were having a great time singing and praising the Lord when a big rig truck from the other lane jackknifed and headed straight toward us. I just remember saying, "Jesus!" The truck hit the car in front of us, and that car went flying. Then the truck veered around us and slammed into the car right behind us. Absolutely nothing happened to us! We miraculously escaped certain death from a head-on collision with a semi! In many ways, that's the moment I answered the call to ministry. Just another time where the devil wanted to crush my life, but God had other plans, plans for me to live and not die. He delivered me from death so I could bring this message of freedom.

The devil will always try to kill your vision in its infancy stage if he can. He tried to kill Moses when he was just a baby. He tried to kill Jesus when he was just a baby. Don't let the devil kill you in your infancy stage. A lot of things that happened to me were in my earlier years when I first started my journey with the Lord. The enemy was trying his hardest to squash the seed of what God had planned for me. Because the devil knows that once you start learning how to walk by faith and learn about your authority, your identity in Him, he will have a harder time taking advantage of you.

GOD REDEEMS THE TIME

I like to challenge people in their early walks, saying, "You didn't get in that mess overnight, and now you will have to work overtime for a while just to balance things out and make up for all that lost time." Paul called it "redeeming the time because the days are evil" (Ephesians 5:16). The word "redeemed" means "to buy back." Time is finite. Nobody can give you more time, nobody. They're not making any more of it.

But be encouraged! God can redeem your time. God can give you years back that were stolen by the enemy. What the devil intended for evil, God redeems for good. Never forget that God has a plan for your life. A plan for you to live and not die!

10

Single and Whole

I remember early on in my walk with God, maybe the first or second year, while living at the group home, I had started dating a girl. It was a pure relationship. We were both committed to not letting our relationship get physical. I think the most we did was hold hands one time.

I was working at the pastor's office at the church we were both attending. One time, as she walked into the office, the Holy Spirit spoke to me as clear as day and said, "Why are you messing around with another man's old lady? She is not your wife. She belongs to another man. She's not the girl for you and you're going to reap what you sow!"

She looked like she had seen a ghost when she looked up and saw me standing across the office. I just blurted out, "I'm so sorry. I don't mean to hurt you, but this relationship is not of God. God has somebody else for you." And He did. A few years later she got married, had kids, and was blessed. I, on the other hand, ended up waiting almost eight more years to get married.

During that time, I discovered that it was possible to be single and whole. I learned how to be single and satisfied. Instead of thinking I always had to have a companion, I knew that God could be my companion. That was a valuable lesson for me to learn; I've since realized that many people don't understand that lesson until it's too late. When they find their spouse, they put pressure on him or her to get something from them that they can only get from God.

Throughout those long years of waiting, God was always so faithful to reassure me, telling me, "I have somebody specifically for you; just be patient." I knew the Bible said, "Do not be unequally yoked together with unbelievers" (2 Corinthians 6:14 NIV). So, it was obvious that God would send me a Christian woman to marry. But what I really thought the Lord was saying to me in that scripture was "not to be yoked together with somebody who has another calling on her life . . . because the reason I'm yoking you with a specific woman *is for a specific assignment.* There's a purpose when I put a yoke on an ox; it is to plow a field. I have a field for you and a field for your future wife, and together you will plow the fields I give you."

So, I waited and waited … and waited. One year, two years, three years, four years, five years, still waiting. Six years, seven years, eight years. It was almost nine years before I met Elizabeth, and the moment I saw her, I knew she would someday be my wife. It was like the stars went off like a fireworks show inside of me. I just knew she was the one.

MEETING ELIZABETH

Jason Lozano and wife, Elizabeth Lozano.

In those days, I was a teacher at Cottonwood School of Ministry, and it just so happened that Elizabeth was a student at Cottonwood at the same time. One time we were both in the foyer area of the school. I was drinking water from the water fountain when she came up to say hi. She had known me through my ministry, but even though we knew many of the same people, we had never met before.

At that time, I was traveling quite a bit, preaching in several of the churches in the region, so I was fairly well-known around the school. So, Elizabeth confidently came up and tapped me on the shoulder and said, "Hi." When I turned around, I played it off like, *I'm the well-known evangelist.* I said, "Hi," you know, sounding all cool and professional on the outside. But on the inside, I was like, *Oh my Lord Jesus! Is she the one?*

I went home that night and told the Lord, "Lord, you know that if I can get a wife without you, I don't want her. I want her to come from you." So I knew there was no way I would get Elizabeth without God's help.

But I knew she was the one. I said, "God, if you give Liz to me, I'll go anywhere you want me to go, Lord." She was well, well worth waiting those eight years for! I went home that night after I talked to her and told my mom, "I saw my wife today!" Later, when I brought Elizabeth to meet my mom, she started crying. Through tears she told me, "That's her." I said, "I told you. I told you. I told you!" So, Elizabeth and I courted, and six months later, when everything was settled, we got married in Westminster, in a beautiful hacienda-style mansion, with a pastor from Cottonwood performing the ceremony.

That's my side of the story, but now I believe it's important for you to hear from Elizabeth, from her perspective.

ELIZABETH'S SIDE OF THE STORY

I got saved when I was seventeen and started attending a youth ministry. The following year when I was eighteen, I went to a crusade in Anaheim, California, taking place outside at a park. I was just sitting there when I noticed this young man walk onto the stage and start preaching, sharing his testimony. I thought to myself, *Wow, his story is so powerful.* Then the young man said a word from God, "Somebody here should have died in a car accident, but God saved and rescued you." I was shocked. He was talking about me! I had just gone through a bad car accident where the car flipped over six times, but I was rescued; it was obviously a miracle from God.

In my heart, at that moment, I had a random thought out of the blue, *I want to marry somebody like that, someone powerful like him.* So, probably at least another year or year and a half passed, and by then, I was going to Cottonwood School of Ministry. I had heard about Jason; Some people had invited me to a few of his events, but I didn't go to many. When I saw him in the foyer, he was getting a drink at the water fountain. In my heart, I thought, *Oh my gosh, he's that guy I heard preaching in the park that time. I remember him!* I think I was just excited by the fact that I remembered him.

Now, I normally wouldn't just go up to someone I didn't know and say, "Hi!" But I tapped him on the shoulder while he was drinking water at the water fountain, and I said, "Hi. I know you; I've seen you before." As I said, I was just excited that I had recognized him. So I started talking to him, saying, "I've heard you preach before, and I think we might know some of the same people."

Looking back, I could tell that I'd startled him. He took a few steps back and got really serious, not at all the way he was up onstage preaching. I thought to myself, *Oh no, I was just excited that I recognized him, but now I think he thinks I like him!*

After that, he would come back every few months to visit Cottonwood, and because we had talked that one time at the water fountain, he would speak with me for ten to fifteen minutes and invite me to any events he had coming up. I would take his flyers and say, "Okay, thank you." But the Lord would never release me to attend one of his events. I really wanted to go but would feel in my heart, *"No, you can't go, don't go."*

Then one day, I had one of his flyers lying on the night-stand in my bedroom while I was living with my mom. The Lord told me, "If you want to marry somebody like that, there's some work I need to do on the inside of your heart." I said, "Okay." So, the Lord began to work with me. He began to tell me, "I want you to let go of some of the friendships you are currently holding on to. I just want you to focus on falling in love with Me." I obeyed and did everything He asked, while still keeping my distance from Jason.

Single and Whole

Over the next few months, Jason and I gradually became friends because of our quick conversations that took place whenever he occasionally visited the school. Then one day, Jason invited me to his church, and without praying about it first I just said, "Okay." But once I got there, the Lord convicted me, "What are you doing? I don't want you getting together with Jason yet." So, without even going into the church, I got back in my car and drove to a local Chili's restaurant, where I had lunch alone. That experience was so good for me because it was like the Lord was telling me, if He was going to put something together, I didn't have to do anything to make it happen.

It wasn't until Jason and I found out that we were both going on the same mission trip that we really started talking and our relationship started to take off. We didn't end up going on the mission trip after all, but we did start dating officially.

Our first date just happened to be on Valentine's Day. He took me to the prayer tower in the Crystal Cathedral in Anaheim. We were sitting there quietly when Jason asked me, "Liz, what is the Lord telling you?" I thought to myself, *Why is he asking me this?* I said, "I don't know, what's the Lord telling you?" He asked me again, "Liz, what is the Lord telling you?" And again I said, "I don't know, what's the Lord telling you?" There was no way I was going to tell him that I liked him or anything like that. Then he said, "Okay, fine. I feel in my heart that you're the one for me." And I said, "Oh yeah, I knew that a long time ago!" He just laughed and laughed. After that, it was pretty simple. Everything just flowed. When we got married, his church was already six months old. So, for a good couple of years I just followed, listened, and watched him. I had a lot to learn about ministry.

A MARRIAGE OF PURPOSE

I was pastoring the church for about six months, and then I married Liz. So, all that happened about the same time: I started the church, met Liz, then we married, and Liz became a pastor's wife. Liz is blessed with an incredible gift of administration. So, it didn't take long for me to realize what God meant when He told me that He was going to yoke me together with a specific woman for a specific assignment, and I knew just what that assignment was.

In the beginning, I gave every ounce of energy I had as a young man into building the church. I put it all out there, and I was worn out. I couldn't give any more. That's when God revealed to me 1 Corinthians 12. One of the gifts listed there is the gift of wise administration, and it seemed to jump off the page at me as I read it. The Lord spoke to me in that moment, "Your wife has that gift, and you're not going any further in your ministry until you release her into that calling because I'm trying to do something out of this gift." I'm more of a visionary, but I tell you, once she stepped into her role as an administrator, the church just exploded, and it has had several seasons of explosive growth since then.

God knows exactly who you're supposed to marry and why. At our church, we do personality profiles, gift tests, and all kinds of tests to find out what people are gifted in, but we had none of that back then. What we did have was the

Holy Ghost, and if you look on paper, Liz and I would be a perfect match for each other. Christian Mingle would have definitively put us together! (Just kidding!) But God was the one who connected us.

A FIGHT OF FAITH

Then, about nine months after we were married, Liz got pregnant with our first child. God had even already given us his name. His name would be Joshua. Then, three or four months into her pregnancy, we went to the doctor for the first time. We had never done anything like that before. We were young, and we were nervous.

We went to the doctor, and they did an ultrasound. Afterward, the doctor called us into his office. We could tell he was really concerned, which made us even more nervous. From the ultrasound, he measured our son's head, and he said our baby wasn't right; then he went further, telling us that we needed to abort him in two weeks, and he set the appointment right away. The doctor even said to us that the pregnancy could be dangerous for Liz. We were shocked. Our hearts just fell. Liz started crying . . . but I started getting mad.

The old, angry, fighting Jason tried to come out on the doctor, but I was able to keep my cool, despite the devasting news. When we got in the car, I turned to Liz and said, "No, Liz, his name is Joshua. God has already given us his name." So, we went home and didn't tell anyone at that time. We were just starting to learn a lot from prominent Word of Faith teachers and I'd already been learning the Word of

Faith from Cottonwood for a few years. I already understood how to walk by faith, and it was that spirit of faith that got us through that season. For two weeks straight, we turned off all distractions, like the TVs in the house, and played recordings of the Word, meditated on the Word, and read all the healing scriptures we could find, over and over again.

These things built our faith tremendously. We believed that we received the miracle of healing for our baby boy. We sowed a seed, we believed God, and by faith, we received our miracle. We had assurance in our hearts that God would take care of him. We didn't know how He was going to do it, but we prayed that God would make our son's head normal.

Two weeks later, we went back to the doctor's office. They did the ultrasound scan again, and the doctor looked shocked, like he'd seen a ghost. He looked at us and said, "I don't know what to tell you. I've never seen this before in my career." While he was talking, I was thinking *I knew it; Go ahead, doctor. You told us to abort our baby. Now . . . tell me what happened. Come on. Come out with it!* Finally, the doctor shook his head and said, "Your baby is normal; He's fine."

Yes, that was a mighty miracle, but the pregnancy continued to be a battle all the way through because the medical team wanted Liz to have a C-section surgery when it came time for her to give birth. The Holy Spirit told me that the devil would try to kill her during the procedure and for us not to do the C-section. Now, I don't recommend ignoring doctors' recommendations for people, but this was personal. I believe in C-sections; there's nothing wrong with them. They're a blessing for so many. Just not for us, not for that time.

Liz pushed for three straight hours, and little Joshua wouldn't come out. They told us just one more push, and if he didn't come out, they would have to perform the C-section. The Holy Spirit reminded me that this could not happen, that the devil would try to kill her.

I told Liz, "Babe, my faith has taken you as far as I can take you. It's all on you now. One more push, one more." That's when I saw my warrior wife emerge; I could see it in her eyes. She took one more deep breath and cried out, "I'm redeemed from the curse of the law! The blessing of Abraham is mine!" And boom, Baby Joshua came right out! What a battle we fought for our firstborn son, Joshua.

Two years later, we conceived again. But when we went to the doctor, we discovered the baby had no heartbeat. We were devastated to learn that we had miscarried. Then we conceived again, and we miscarried again. Then we knew that the battle was on. We were tempted to get bitter and think, *Where are you, God? This faith stuff doesn't work.* Fortunately, we had already renewed our minds, and knew that this was not like our God. Our God is a good God, the enemy is the enemy, and we just asked God to give us wisdom. He did it. He helped us. He gave us strength, wisdom, and faith.

We conceived again and God gave us the name of our baby. He said her name would be Joy. And "she will come in the morning" (Psalm 30:5) and with that word, that "rhema," we went to battle for Joy. I remember this vividly. Liz is the worship leader at our church, but one Sunday, she came home early, and I could tell something was wrong. She had been in church all day, and now she was coming home during worship, crying. Something was definitely wrong. She was feeling all the symptoms of miscarriage again.

So, I said, "Babe, lay down. I'm going to go preach." I remember preaching and taking authority and preaching my way through it. Then Joy did come in the morning, our baby daughter. Those are the battles for our first two children, but for my third son, God told me his name would be Noah, and he would bring our family peace because it was a battle for our first two children. But Noah came easy, and he did bring us peace. He's our prophet.

GOD NAMES OUR CHILDREN

Many have asked me what I mean when I say the Lord showed me my children's names before they were born. They want to know exactly how He does that. I'm sure God does it differently with different people, but with me, it always came with reading the Bible. As I was reading through the Bible, the name just popped out, like when God showed me that Liz had the gift of administration. For me, the scripture actually stands out from the page. For example, imagine the font on the page you are reading is a 10-point font. With me, that font becomes bold, and jumps to a 24-point. And then, in my heart, I hear, *"Joshua."* In my heart, I hear, *"Joy, and she will come in the morning."* In my heart, I hear, *"Noah, and he will bring the family peace."*

Noah was the hardest name of the three to get. It was almost at the end of the pregnancy, and we didn't have a name yet! So we were like, "Come on, God, what's his name?" But God was faithful and each of my three kids were named while still in the womb.

11

Small Beginnings

In the book of Zechariah, there's a popular verse that says in part, " . . . Not by might, nor by power, but by my spirit, saith the Lord of hosts" (Zechariah 4:6 KJV). But just a few verses down, there's another verse that's just as powerful and important as verse 6. Verse 10 says, "Do not despise these small beginnings, for the Lord rejoices to see the work begin . . ." (Zechariah 4:10).

I often teach on this scripture: the Kingdom of God always starts with a seed, then grows, and becomes a great covering. Over the years, God has taught us not to despise the days of small beginnings. Today, the church I pastor, Freedom City Church, is big, running well over five thousand people in attendance every weekend . . . but it didn't start that way.

BLUEBIRD ART LOUNGE

As I mentioned a couple of chapters ago, back in 2003, I felt the call from God to return to Whittier and start a church. Only God knew where that calling would lead. I started the church in a tiny dive called the Bluebird Art Lounge. The small space only fit maybe twenty chairs, and in the summer-time, temperatures would soar to 120 degrees or more in the stifling room.

It was brutal. And back then, the worship band was just one guy, a musician (I'm not kidding about humble begin-nings!). He was a good worship leader. He's doing great now, but at the time, he was addicted to crack cocaine. As I mentioned earlier, I would pray for him, get him free, and he would do good for a while, but then he'd disappear and I'd have to go find him and bring him back. Sometimes it'd be Sunday morning before our 2:00 p.m. service, and I'd have to go get him. I'd find him and discover he'd been up all night. I'd pray for him, get him cleaned up, and say, "Let's go." I'll admit that it's a pretty crazy way to do church, but that's pioneering. When you're pioneering, you use anything (or anybody) you can. Eventually, that guy got free from cocaine and became a successful businessman. He got married and had kids and his whole life turned around.

Our children's ministry was out in the back alley, complete with oil stains on the pavement, and dumpsters full of trash. Our sound system was borrowed, everything was makeshift. The Bluebird Art Lounge was supposed to be an eclectic art lounge, but it was full of junk. It was horrible, but that's where we started, and I was very grateful for it. Talk about humble beginnings!

The lady who owned the property had another tiny unit, just five hundred or six hundred square feet. We used that for a foyer. Another little area next to it, which was only about four hundred or five hundred square feet, I knocked down that dividing wall to give us just a little more room. The monthly budget for the Bluebird was $400 a month, and when I jumped in, I jumped in all the way. I quit my job and collected unemployment for six months. I think our first offering was a whopping $27! That was how the Freedom International Christian Training Center got its start.

By the way, that's still the church's full name today, but we don't put that out publicly. We use "Freedom City Church" publicly because the longer name tends to confuse people. They think we're a training center or school, not a church. But I had a clear vision from the Lord that the church would go international and that it was supposed to be a training center and a church. So it has done that and become that kind of training ministry, but at first, the name confused many people. Is this a church? Is this a center? Another cool part about our story is that today our new building is just two blocks away from the old Bluebird Art Lounge where we started.

GROWING . . . AND MOVING UP!

It didn't take long for us to outgrow the tiny Bluebird, and soon we were looking for a larger place to meet. Our second building was in Whittier, also on Washington Boulevard. To make it work, we formed a partnership with a church member. We went in together with every penny we had; He started a counseling center in the space and I started the church. It was a counseling center during the day and a church at night and on the weekends. It was 1,500 square feet and a huge cost for the budget. We split the monthly rent in half, so we went from paying $400 for the Bluebird to $800 for the larger space, which was a big stretch for us. We didn't have any money to get anything. Our first stage was made from old wooden pallets I had dug out of some alley. We screwed them together, put plywood decking down, and finished it off by wrapping it in some carpet. That became our very first stage, all creaky, uneven, and prone to breaking apart.

Somebody donated some old pews that another church was throwing away, so we were able to replace those cheap, ugly, pink chairs that we used in the Bluebird. But the pews weren't much better looking; they were an ugly shade of blue. Next, we found somebody who was throwing away a bunch of old carpeting that we were able to piece together to cover the floor in the church.

That was how we had to do church initially, in the early, pioneering days. But then, the church really started to grow. I remember the devil would lie to me, saying we'd never get past a hundred people. But I remember the Sunday when we finally broke one hundred people, which was the capacity of that building. At that point, thanks to a miracle from God, we were able to raise some money so we could afford to move into the larger building next door. We got some decent carpeting, some more comfortable chairs, and a bit of a nicer stage. We even got a projector, but we couldn't afford a screen, so we painted one of the concrete walls bright white and used that as a screen. We spent every dime we had to get the building ready for church the following Sunday; We were finally ready to open the doors.

GOD MOVES!

It was Friday afternoon, and the property manager came by to look at what we'd done. She didn't like it for some reason and made it clear that she didn't like us either! She even cussed me out, saying, "I'm kicking you out of here!" She really had it out for us. She continued her rant, "Monday, I'm kicking you out." I told her, "But the owner gave me permission to do the work!" "But *I* didn't give you permission." That didn't make any sense to me. The owner had told me I could do the work, and now this woman was telling me, "But *I* didn't tell you, so *I'm* kicking you out on Monday."

Believe me, I wasn't looking forward to standing up in front of the church, preaching, then having to tell the people that everything we'd worked so hard for was over. So I went to God, "God, you told me to tell Pharaoh to let my people go." I reminded God of what He told me when He called me to start the church. And I just prayed. I prayed and prayed, that's all I did. Then I got up and preached on Sunday, and I decided not to tell the church; I didn't feel led to do it. So I just preached, then closed in prayer.

Monday came around and the property manager never showed up. Tuesday came around, and she never showed up. It wasn't until four days later that the owner showed up and said, "Hey, the manager is no longer here. Is there anything you need?" I said, "No, we're happy. She sure was upset with me, though." And he told me, "Don't worry about her; I fired her." "Really?" I said. "Yeah, last Friday night." Evidently, about the time we were praying, a fire had broken out in one of the other units that the guy owned. Ultimately, he determined that the fire was the property manager's fault and fired her. It was like God saying to us, "I have your back." From there, we continued to grow and eventually took over another unit that the guy owned, and that's when another miracle occurred.

A "JUST IN TIME" MIRACLE

The business partner I had at the time lacked integrity. I didn't realize it then, but he was pocketing all the money I was giving him for the rent and utilities. This had been going on for six months, totaling about $10,000. Finally, he asked me one day, "Hey, do you want the building?" I told him we did because we were getting too big and needed the space he was using as the counseling center on weekdays.

I couldn't really afford it, but I took a step of faith. I said, "Yes, I'll take it." Even though it was out of our budget, I knew I could take a salary cut, figuring we'd cut back because we really needed the extra space. The guy gave me the keys and told me, "The bills are right here in this stack, along with a list of when they're all due. Everything you need is right there." I said, "Okay, great." But when I started investigating, I realized he hadn't paid the rent, utilities, or anything else for six months!

So, there I was with no money in the bank, barely making it, and I've got a bill for $10,000, and it's due. So again, I went to God and said, "God, you told me to start this church. I didn't know this guy was stealing money from us. I need your help!" I finished praying, then said, "Okay, there's nothing more we can do. It's Monday. We don't have the money, and the bank closes at 5:00 p.m."

I decided to do what every man of God does when times get tough; I took the family to Disneyland! We didn't have any money at the time, but my wife's mom and her family worked at Disneyland, so they gave us free passes. So, we were on our way to Disneyland!

But before leaving, I got a phone call from an old friend named Dan. I hadn't talked to Dan in years. We had become close friends in the rehab program years before, and when he got out, he'd moved to Texas, and I'd lost track of him. Now out of the blue, he called me and asked, "How are you doing, Jason?" I said, "Wow, Dan, I guess I'm doing okay." I didn't tell him that we were about to lose the church. Then, he said, "I heard you're starting a church." I told him I was. He said, "Well, I want to help you. I sold my house in Texas and I want to move back to Los Angeles to help you." I said, "Okay, great!"

Then he says, "I sold my house, and I'm in town and have a check I want to give you. When can I get it to you?" I knew immediately that this was a God moment. I told him I could meet him right now. So, I turned around from heading to Disneyland and went straight to meet Dan. I knew time was tight, it was getting close to 5:00 p.m., and the bank was about to close.

I pulled up to meet him, and we hadn't seen each other in years. I could tell he wanted to spend some time catching up, and I was so grateful for his generosity, but I also knew I would have to get his check to the bank . . . quickly. He gave me a big hug and asked, "Hey, how are you doing?" I was like, "Great, great," all the while thinking about the bank closing. So, he gave me the check, pulled out another one, and said, "This one's for you, your wife, and your family." I told him, "Man, I love you, and I'm so grateful for this gift, but I need to go get this in the bank!" On the way to the bank I opened the envelope and looked at the check, and it was for exactly the amount we needed, $10,000!

Once again, it was like God reminding us, "I'm with you." The amount Dan gave was no more or no less than what we needed. We were able to pay all we owed. From there, we took the next building and the next. We eventually took over the whole complex. Then we outgrew that place and needed to grow again.

So, at this time, I didn't know that you couldn't build a church without the city's permission. You need permits, inspections, approvals, and a whole host of things I had no idea about. We needed a new building and I had been looking for a bigger space, but then the city slapped an ordinance on the doors of our existing space saying we couldn't occupy it as a church. I thought, *What am I going to do, God?* I got in my car and started driving around the city, looking for a building. There wasn't an available church building anywhere. Nowadays, in Los Angeles, one of the hardest things to find is a church.

So, I was driving around town looking for a church. It's important to note that I wasn't looking for "For Sale" signs but for signs from the Lord. I was listening to my heart, not looking with my eyes. Eventually, I found a great space that we could use for a church. It was in an old warehouse. It was a miracle that I was able to find it. Again, I was listening to the Lord, and when I drove past this warehouse, God said, "Act." So, I called the building owner immediately.

When we started negotiating the price, I told him, "I'll just give you what you're asking."

At the time, I had no idea there were two or three other people in position to get the building. They had called ahead of me, but they were trying to finagle the price lower. So, when I called and offered to pay his asking price, he jumped at the offer, and we were able to get the building.

The pastors who had called ahead of me ended up getting buildings better suited for their ministries, so in the end, everyone came out a winner. So, you see, every step of the way, the hand of God was gently leading and guiding us along, showing us where to go. But we were not done growing. God was teaching us from very early on not just to make the bricks; God wanted us to own the bricks.

A SURPRISE VOTE

We grew out of the warehouse location and had to move to our campus in Santa Fe Springs. We had to battle a real Goliath there. I think the devil knew what was going to happen, and he just fought us every step of the way. The church that was meeting in the location before us had built it in such a way that they didn't get the proper permits. Consequently, when we took our plans to the city, they wouldn't zone it because our plans didn't allow for enough parking. But they told us that even if there would have been enough space for parking, they weren't going to zone it because of the previous outstanding permits. It was as if they had already made up their minds to deny us the zoning we needed.

We had to go back and forth with the city several times to plead our case. Finally, they brought it up for a vote, and miraculously, they granted us the exact zoning we needed! It was another supernatural move of God! They changed an ordinance just for our church, something that had never been done before in the city's history. It was just the favor of God.

From that moment, the church just blew up, and it exploded with rapid growth. We were there at the Santa Fe Springs campus for about ten years, taking part of that city block, about twenty thousand square feet, which is big here in our area. We had services on Sundays at 9:00 a.m., 11:00 a.m., 1:00 p.m., 3:00 p.m., 5:00 p.m., and a 7:00 p.m. service. I preached five of those services for many years.

GOING FULL CIRCLE

Then one Sunday, right in the middle of a water baptism service, the Lord spoke to me. He said, "I need you to go back to Whittier," which is right next to where we were in Santa Fe Springs. I knew what that meant. God wanted us to go full circle and move back to the area where the Bluebird Art Lounge was originally, Uptown Whittier.

So, we began our search for another building, and once again, it was not easy to find what we needed. Finally, one day we were at a hotel we were considering renting when a woman overheard our conversation. She approached us and asked if we were looking for a church. We said we were, and she told us, "I'm not from around here, but my brother is from here, and he had a church that met at the YMCA, but they just moved to another building. I'm not sure, but the YMCA might be available. You should go talk to the director over there." So, we met with the director of the YMCA, and sure enough, the building was available, so we moved over there and started having services. That was a pivotal move because it set us up just one block away from the building we're in now.

When we got to the YMCA, once again, we had tremendous favor. God has always been faithful to provide exactly what we needed and when we needed it. Eventually, we grew out of the space at the YMCA, and God did another huge miracle to get us into the property where we are today.

COMING HOME TO A BRILLIANT LOCATION

There are two significant historic buildings in our city. There's the Nixon Building and the old city hall, where our church meets right now. These two buildings are the oldest, most historic buildings in the city of Whittier, California. Our building has always been a church, but it also used to be the Whittier City Hall during the week.

These two properties are on the corner of Greenleaf and Hadley. Our church meets in a beautiful building and in a beautiful location. The building really is priceless.

And God continues to provide. When we're all finished, the auditorium will hold one thousand people, and we'll be able to fit another six hundred in the overflow areas.

But the true brilliance of this building is not found in the auditorium, where we already hold five services every Sunday, all filled to capacity. No, the absolute brilliance of this building is the seventy-five thousand square feet of classroom space we now have, which is how we choose to do ministry. The core of what we do is training.

Today, we have training centers where about eighty young men and women are being discipled for ministry. We've also opened up recovery homes. Then we have about four thousand people participating in five hundred to six hundred small groups each week. In addition, we have about 1,600 students enrolled in our various schools and well over five thousand people in our congregation. Our ministry has gone all over the world. In our "Lifestyle of Freedom" program, we have students from twenty-six different countries. Today, because of God's faithfulness, we are what we named the church many years ago, an "international Christian training center." We've certainly come a long way since the days in the Bluebird Art Lounge!

GODLY PRINCIPLES FOR LIFE

You may not need a church building for what God's called you to do, but you can still follow the godly principles that I try my best to walk out in my life:

- **Never forget that God has a plan for your life.** That's so important. I want to repeat it. God has a specific plan just for you. You can put your hope in that. You have a purpose and meaning in this life. Read Jeremiah 29:11 and pray that God will reveal His perfect plan to you!

- **Don't limit God.** So many people get in trouble because they think too small. Remember, "God is able to do much more than you can ask or even think" (Ephesians 3:20)! Pray big prayers!

- **Our God speaks!** So "pray, and let your needs be made known to Him" (Philippians 4:6). Then don't forget to listen! Don't come out of your prayer closet until you have a word from God.

- **Don't let anything or anybody deter you from doing what God has called you to do.**

- **Once you put your hand on that promise, you go forward.** There's no looking back. "Anyone who puts a hand to the plow and then looks back is not fit for the Kingdom of God" (Luke 9:62).

- **Never give up!** "For the kingdom of heaven suffers violence, and violent men will take it by force" (Matthew 11:12 ESV).

12

Forever Free

From the moment I was called into the ministry, my charge from God has not changed one degree. He has called me to boldly stand up and confront the pharaohs of this world, those spiritual forces in high places that are controlling people, oppressing them, binding them up in slavery, trapping them in their sin.

I am perfectly suited for my calling; I know what it's like to be held in bondage to sin. I know what it's like to be enslaved, shackled not only by my evil actions but by my limited-thinking mind as well. The devil had control of my mind, and I was oppressed by him all day every day. I was one of his soldiers, winning many victories for the kingdom of darkness, enslaving others who were just like me, lost and afraid.

But, as you've read, God loved me enough to come and rescue me from my dark place. He pulled me up out of the miry clay and set my feet on solid ground. The Lord set me free! But that's not all. God called me for a purpose. He had a plan for my life, a plan for good and not for evil, to prosper me and not to harm me, a plan to give me a hope and a future (Jeremiah 29:11). I've been sent out with a single message, burning in my heart, for the oppressing Pharaohs of this world. The King of kings and the Lord of lords says, "Set my people free!" The Lord of hosts has one message for the kingdom of darkness, "Let my people go!"

I pray every day that I'm being faithful to my calling. The ministry is certainly bearing lots of good fruit. The Lord has built Freedom City Church to well over five thousand people here in Los Angeles.

Opening of Freedom City Church in Whittier, CA in 2023.

Our goal is to have thousands of leaders. So at the rate the church is growing now, we'll have over thirty thousand people in ten years. That's big enough to create a real impact, to make a significant difference, influencing the lives of those living in this city.

Eventually, I see a total of ten campuses here in the L.A. area, and we're going to take Los Angeles for Jesus Christ. That's what I see in the future, eventually planting churches all over the world. Why? To make our name great? Certainly not! We want to expand because the message of freedom is so needed right now across the world. We want to make *His* name great!

In order to stay healthy even with rapid growth, we will have to multiply our leaders and new campuses, establishing new church sites worldwide, and raising up pastors all along the way. Yes, we're on our way. We already have our building which is like a big shopping center with one hundred twenty thousand square feet of space. It's perfect for raising up an army! And everywhere we establish a new campus, God is setting the captives free!

Freedom City Church

God is in the business of setting captives free and redeeming what was once lost. To think that the location of our church right now is in the very same area where I experienced more abuse than I ever experienced in my life. And it's also where I committed most of the crimes and the terrible things I did. It's literally all right there in that same area. I'm just so glad that our God is a God who redeems! You can believe that promise no matter who you are or what you've done. God redeems the lost and the broken. The stories of my life are a testimony to that fact.

What about you? Have you hit rock bottom? Have you had enough of slavery and bondage? Whatever your story may be, I can promise you that God is with you. He's right there beside you with a beautiful plan to save you, redeem your life, and set you free. Pharaoh has been commanded to loosen his icy grip on your life and let you go. God is just waiting for you to ask Him to set you free. And once He sets you free, you are free indeed!

Jason Lozano with his wife, Elizabeth, eldest son, Joshua, daughter, Joy, and youngest son, Noah.

SCAN QR
FOR MORE
INFORMATION

AUTHOR CONTACT

Jason Lozano
P.O. Box 739
Whittier, CA 90608
(562) 278-2108
Jasonlozano.org
Info@jasonlozano.org

Follow Jason Lozano on YouTube and Instagram!
@Jasonlozano